D0968586

DIY Financial Advisor

Founded in 1807, John Wiley & Sons is the oldest independent publishing company in the United States. With offices in North America, Europe, Australia, and Asia, Wiley is globally committed to developing and marketing print and electronic products and services for our customers' professional and personal knowledge and understanding.

The Wiley Finance series contains books written specifically for finance and investment professionals, as well as sophisticated individual investors and their financial advisers. Book topics range from portfolio management to e-commerce, risk management, financial engineering, valuation and financial instrument analysis, as well as much more.

For a list of available titles, visit our website at www.WileyFinance.com.

DIY Financial Advisor

A Simple Solution to Build and Protect Your Wealth

WESLEY R. GRAY, PhD,
JACK R. VOGEL, PhD,
DAVID P. FOULKE

WILEY

Published by John Wiley & Sons, Inc., Hoboken, New Jersey.
Published simultaneously in Canada.

For general information on our other products and services or for technical support, please contact our Customer Care Department within the United States at (800) 762-2974, outside the United States at (317) 572-3993 or fax (317) 572-4002.

Wiley also publishes its books in a variety of electronic formats. Some content that appears in print may not be available in electronic books. For more information about Wiley products, visit our website at www.wiley.com.

Library of Congress Cataloging-in-Publication Data

Gray, Wesley R.
 DIY financial advisor : a simple solution to build and protect your wealth / Wesley R. Gray, PhD, Jack R. Vogel, PhD, and David P. Foulke.
    pages cm. – (Wiley finance series)
  Includes index.
  ISBN 978-1-119-07150-1 (cloth) — ISBN 978-1-119-12491-7 (epdf) – ISBN 978-1-119-12490-0 (epub)
 1. Portfolio management. 2. Families–Economic aspects. 3. Wealth–Management. 4. Investment advisors. I. Vogel, Jack R., 1983- II. Foulke, David P., 1966- III. Title.
  HG4529.5.G736 2015
  332.024–dc23
                                                                                          2015013795

Cover Design: Wiley
Cover Images: Investment charts with laptop © Nonwarit/Shutterstock;
Market graph, dollars and calculator © iStock.com/Niyazz

Printed in the United States of America

10 9 8 7 6 5 4 3 2

For those investors looking to get empowered through education.

—Wes, Jack, and David

Contents

Preface

This book is a synopsis of our research findings developed while serving as a consultant and asset manager for large family offices. By way of background, a family office is a company, or group of people, who manage the wealth a family has gained over generations. The term *family office* has an element of cachet, and even mystique, because it is usually associated with the mega-wealthy. However, practically speaking, virtually any family that manages its investments—independent of the size of the investment pool—could be considered a family office. The difference is mainly semantic. For example, the term *individual investor* is often a reference to the head of a household who manages a family's assets. This "individual investor" is a de facto family office—no matter whether this individual investor manages a $10,000 portfolio or a $5,000,000,000 portfolio. The goal is the same as for even the largest family office.

There are benefits and costs to being a family office. The key advantage a family office or, by extension, any individual investor, has over so-called "institutional" investors, is the ability to make long-term investment decisions that maximize after-tax, after-fee risk-adjusted performance, without fear of a misalignment of incentives—those who own the money are the best stewards of the money. By contrast, a professional institutional investor, or "hired gun," is crippled by a misalignment between the incentives of the owners of capital and those of the investment manager, who has a separate incentive to keep his job, which can create a shorter-term perspective that can conflict with a long-term perspective. The decision that maximizes the after-fee, after-tax, risk-adjusted returns on capital, while optimal for the owner of capital, is not always the optimal decision for a third-party investment manager.

The key disadvantages for a family office, or an individual investor, relative to an institutional investor, are the effect of taxes and a knowledge gap that is sometimes more closely related to perception than reality. But fear not; this book is meant to fill the knowledge gap by providing the reader with the tools to be successful and the confidence to minimize the use of "experts." And taxes, while challenging, can be minimized by limiting trading activity, engaging in smart planning, and by following some of the simple rules we outline in this book.

Perhaps you are skeptical that you can manage your own wealth. After all, legions of wealth managers have probably told you repeatedly that you cannot. We are here to tell you that you can. We have been lucky to work with and learn from some superb family offices, and the people that run their organizations. The main finding from our experience is that complexity does not imply value—especially when talking about investments.

Many less wealthy investors are told that the mega-rich benefit from their access to arcane strategies, hedge funds, and private equity invest-ments. We are here to tell you that this popular and widespread meme has been propagated by salesmen, not by evidence: access to overpriced, opaque, complex, tax-inefficient exposures typically managed by egomaniacs is not an advantage—it is a serious disadvantage!

What matters in investing are avoiding psychology traps and sticking to the FACTS (fees, access, complexity, taxes, and search), a framework we describe in Chapter 5. These simple concepts apply to everyone, not just the ultra-wealthy. The findings of this book are therefore applicable to the middle-class as well as to the mega-rich. Attempting to maintain and grow wealth accumulated over a lifetime is a task that is equally daunting for both individuals and for big name family offices.

Our natural inclination is to succumb to the challenge of portfolio man-agement and let an "expert" deal with the problem. For a variety of reasons we discuss in this book, we should resist this urge to go with our gut instinct. We suggest that investors maintain direct control, or at least a thorough understanding, of how their hard-earned wealth is managed.

Our book is meant to be an educational journey that slowly builds con-fidence in one's own ability to manage a portfolio. In our book, we explore a potential solution that can be applicable to a wide-variety of investors, from the ultra-high-net-worth to middle-class individual, all of whom are focused on similar goals of preserving and growing their capital over time.

Acknowledgments

We have had enormous support from many colleagues, friends, and family in making this book a reality. We thank our wives, Katie Gray, Meg Vogel, and Eliza Foulke for their continual support and for managing our chaotic kids so we could write our manuscript. We'd also like to thank the entire team at Alpha Architect, for dealing with the three of us while we drafted the initial manuscript. Tian Yao, Yang Xu, Tao Wang, Pat Cleary, Carl Kanner, and Xin Song—we are forever indebted! We'd also like to thank outside readers for their early comments: Sam Lee at Morningstar, Ben Carlson at AWealthofCommonSense.com, and Sam Taylor at Fidelity Investments. Finally, Edward Stern and his team at Hartz Capital, and Bob Kanner and his team at PUBCO, have been invaluable mentors in our endeavor to understand how one should operate a family office.

One

Why You Can Beat the Experts

This book is organized into two parts. Part One sets out the rationale and evidence supporting simple, systematic processes. We begin by questioning society's reliance on "expert" opinion. Highlighting the evidence behind the performance of expert opinion, we explain why experts are self-interested and (surprise) are prone to the same behavioral biases that afflict all human beings. Finally, we highlight that experts often rely on stories, not facts.

Part Two outlines how individual investors, managing from $50 thousand to $5 billion, can beat the experts. We outline the reasons why a do-it-yourself (DIY) approach makes sense. Next, we outline various asset allocation frameworks and explain why a simple approach is probably most effective. Next, following this discussion, we explore simple evidence-based risk-management concepts, which help a DIY investor avoid large losses when investing his capital. Next, we outline ways in which a DIY investor can develop a systematic approach to add value to his equity portfolios by incorporating simple value-based and momentum-based security selection techniques. We then highlight techniques to implement approaches to momentum-based security selection processes. We move on to simple asset allocation frameworks, and we end with a discussion of simple, evidence-based risk-management concepts. Finally, we end Part Two by integrating the knowledge discussed on asset allocation, risk-management, and security selection into a full-fledged investment program with an overview of what we believe to be a reasonable DIY Financial Advisor solution.

CHAPTER 1

Are Experts Trying Too Hard?

"A speculator can always be beset by an unfathomable event—a constellation of unpredictable and unforeseen events—that leads to a disaster that seemingly was impossible, and it's always important to keep this in mind."
—Victor Niederhoffer, Commenting on the 1997 Asian Crisis[1]

It took Victor Niederhoffer many years of study and a lot of hard work to become widely known as an expert in financial markets. After graduating from Harvard and receiving his PhD in finance from the University of Chicago, he continued his ascent within academia, teaching at Berkeley for five years. As an academic, he authored numerous research papers on market anomalies and how one might profit from following clever trading strategies.

As Niederhoffer learned more, and became increasingly sophisticated, he sensed an opportunity to use his academic knowledge to make money. Retiring from academia in 1980, he chose to pursue a career as a practitioner in financial markets. His firm, Niederhoffer Investments, was so successful that he caught the notice of investing guru George Soros. Niederhoffer began working with Soros in the 1980s, advising him on commodities and fixed-income trading. Eventually, Soros allocated $100 million to his firm. During the early 1990s, it was rumored in the financial press that Niederhoffer had been generating returns of 30 percent, or more, *per year*.

In 1996, based on an illustrious track record and a distinguished trading career, Niederhoffer published his personal cookbook, *The Education of a Speculator*, in which he revealed his approach to trading and making money in the markets. Who couldn't learn from this titan of finance? And he was a titan. When his book hit the shelves, Niederhoffer was among the best-known hedge fund managers in the United States, was at the pinnacle of his profession, and had become known as one of the foremost experts on investing worldwide. Niederhoffer was not only an expert, he was an expert's expert.

And so, in 1997, as a widely respected expert in financial markets, Niederhoffer may have been surprised when he experienced steep losses on a Thai currency bet. But Niederhoffer had experienced volatility before; he just needed to apply his prodigious investing skill and pull yet another rabbit out of a hat. While Niederhoffer had fallen behind during early 1997, his real problems began when he chose a risky strategy to recover from those losses: He began selling out-of-the-money puts on the S&P 500.[2]

Selling out-of-the-money puts has been likened to picking up nickels in front of a steamroller. You get a little bit of money (the nickel) for the contract, but you agree to purchase a stock at a future price (the steamroller). Everything works so long as the steam roller doesn't accelerate. However, should our steam roller operator drop his sandwich and inadvertently step on the gas (decrease the stock price), you could find yourself in a pressing situation ...

This pressing situation can become downright perilous when market prices approach or fall below the put strike price. If you promise to buy a stock for $10 and its price on the open market is $5, you can be sure that your creditors will come to collect. And if you can't honor your promise to fulfill the contract, well, that's when you need to worry about the steamroller.

In late October, Niederhoffer's out-of-the-money November puts were trading at $0.60, but the Asian financial crisis continued to unfold and began to rattle US markets. The value of his puts quadrupled to $2.40, although they were still over 15 percent out of the money. Niederhoffer was confident, stayed the course, and left his position intact (he had come back from worse than this).

The following week, the S&P plunged by 7 percent, and the implied volatility of the puts skyrocketed. The puts were both closer to being "in the money" *and* had more implied volatility (the market believed the chance of them ending in the money was greater). Each of these effects made them more expensive. With this put valuation double-whammy, the value of Niederhoffer's puts exploded, which was very bad, since Niederhoffer had sold them. In just over a week's time, Niederhoffer's short position had moved against him by a factor of 25 times or more. This extreme move proved to be too much, even for the master. Shortly thereafter, Niederhoffer had a margin call that he could not meet; his fund's account had gone bankrupt.[3] Cue the steamroller.

How can it be that Victor Niederhoffer—a noted academic, a respected financial expert, a lion on Wall Street, and a financial press darling—could bankrupt his fund by pursuing a volatile options strategy that first year business school students are cautioned against as being too risky? And what did this say about Niederhoffer's expertise?

Some might argue that once Niederhoffer took losses on his Thai currency bet, his incentives changed and affected his perspective. Facing such losses, perhaps this risky option strategy seemed like a reasonable response. Perhaps it was at this point that Niederhoffer became a slave to his emotions, and therefore ceased to be an expert. Perhaps he simply believed in his innate abilities. Perhaps he just wanted to take on more risk. We will never know.

Yet we rely on experts like Niederhoffer because they are supposed to have superior knowledge! They, given their expert credentials, should reach the right conclusion more often than we, the nonexperts. Once Niederhoffer went bust, surely his expert credentials were revoked by the masses and relegated to nonexpert status, right?

Mustafa Zaida, a professional investor who ran a European hedge fund, apparently didn't think so. In 2002, Zaida seeded a new offshore fund called the Matador Fund, with Niederhoffer directing the trading activities. Zaida reportedly commented, "He's definitely learned his lesson." It's hard to know exactly what Zaida's thinking was here, but he clearly believed Niederhoffer still maintained at least some degree of expertise.

The Matador Fund performed well initially, compounding at high rates for several years and growing to $350 million. Then in 2007, during the credit crisis, Matador reportedly lost more than 75 percent of its value. As had happened in 1997, Niederhoffer's account was liquidated. He had "blown up" for the second time in about a decade.[4] And while these episodes were highly public, there are less public rumors that Niederhoffer blew up a third time, although we don't know whether to give much credence to such rumors.

Regardless, for fairly extended periods of time, Niederhoffer definitely appeared to be an expert; he generated high returns, seemingly without excessive downside risk. But did he eliminate the possibility of extreme downside outcomes? No. This was emphatically not the case, as he empirically demonstrated his ability to be steamrolled, not once, but twice.

Some might argue that if Niederhoffer told investors, "You may lose all your money pursuing this strategy, but it will give you high returns," then they were not really relying on his expertise to protect them from bankruptcy. But perhaps this is beside the point. If you are aware of a strategy that compounds at 30 percent, but you know that every few years there will be a year when you lose all of your money, then that is not a strategy worth pursuing. Any expert who recommends such a strategy should not be considered an expert in financial matters.

Of course, there is an alternative explanation here. Maybe Niederhoffer wasn't an expert at all. Maybe Niederhoffer just chose risky strategies that made him look like a genius while they were working, but when he blew up, he demonstrated that he wasn't doing anything special at all. The emperor was revealed to have no clothes. All the fancy academic pedigrees, the studies and papers, the published book, the high returns—in short, all the things that made Niederhoffer an "expert," were perhaps really just an illusion. Perhaps there really was no "expertise" involved, whatsoever. Certainly, after several bankruptcies, that conclusion seems reasonable.

Of course, this story is not meant to pick on Niederhoffer. Like all experts, Niederhoffer is only human. But as we will highlight over the next few chapters, humans are systematically flawed. And so if humans are systematically flawed, why do we still rely on experts for all of our most important decisions?

WHY DO WE RELY ON EXPERTS?

"If you do fundamental trading, one morning you feel like a genius, the next day you feel like an idiot … by 1998 I decided we would go 100% models … we slavishly follow the model. You do whatever it [the model] says no matter how smart or dumb you think it is. And that turned out to be a wonderful business."
                        —Jim Simons, Founder, Renaissance Technologies[5]

Let's start off by examining our coauthor, Wes Gray, a person many would consider an "expert." In fact, in many respects, Wes is eerily similar to Vic Niederhoffer. Wes graduated from an uber-prestigious undergraduate business program at the Wharton School of the University of Pennsylvania and earned an MBA and a PhD in finance from the University of Chicago—sound familiar? Well, it should: This is essentially the same academic training as Vic Niederhoffer.

Upon completion of his PhD, Wes entered academia and spent four years as a full-time tenure-track professor. Wes resigned his post as a full-time academic because he raised almost $200 million in assets from a multibillion-dollar family office and a handful of other ultra-high-net-worth families. This is all uncannily similar to how Niederhoffer started his career. Vic also did his time as a professor, and then left academia after a billionaire (i.e., Soros) gave him a large slug of capital. Let's hope the similarity in the stories between Vic and Wes ends at this stage. The last thing Wes wants to do is blow up multiple asset management firms and lose investor capital. He is also deathly afraid of steamrollers.

Clearly, some people believe Wes is an "expert" and are willing to let him manage a large amount of capital without a multi-decade track record. But why might investors' future experiences differ between Vic and Wes? On paper, the two Chicago finance PhDs are virtually the same. It has been said that the definition of insanity is doing the same thing over and over again and expecting a different outcome. So should we avoid an expert like Wes because he is essentially a carbon copy of Vic?

We think the key difference between Wes and Vic is not related to their financial expertise. The difference is related to their skepticism with regard to their own expertise. On most discretionary, day-to-day aspects of investing, for example, picking individual stock picks or the direction of interest rates, Wes believes firmly that he is completely wrong almost all of the time, whereas Vic believed he could master the markets. And while an expert with no faith in his or her ability sounds counterintuitive, it is actually invaluable because this approach to being an expert minimizes the chance for overconfidence. In fact, Wes has established internal firm structures to ensure that he is reminded on a frequent basis that he is a terrible expert in this sense. But why would an expert systematically convince himself that he is not an expert? The reason Wes engages in this peculiar behavior is explained in a quote often attributed to Mark Twain, "It ain't what we don't know that causes us problems; it's what we know for sure that simply ain't so."

An expert, or any market participant, must acknowledge his own fallibility and must constantly remind himself why he is flawed. This is very difficult to do consistently, since our natural inclination is to believe we are better than average. Unfortunately, on average, we are only going to be average. The ability to question one's own convictions, even when they are firmly held, turns out to be a very useful thing in investing.

The next example highlights how our minds can tell us something with 100 percent confidence, when in fact, what our mind is telling us is 100 percent incorrect.

Figure 1.1 highlights this point.[6] Stare at box A and box B in the figure. If you are a human being you will identify that box A is darker than box B.

Then ask yourself:

"How much would I bet that A is darker than B?" Would you bet $5? $20? $100?

Or perhaps you would borrow money from a bank, and leverage your bet up 10 times and bet $1,000,000 on this bet. Why not, right? It is a *guarantee*.

Edward H. Adelson

FIGURE 1.1 Ed Adelson Checkerboard Illusion

We know how a human approaches this question, but how does a computer think about this question? A computer identifies the red-green-blue (RGB) values for a pixel in box A and the RGB values for a pixel in B. Next, the computer tabulates the results: 120-120-120 for box A; 120-120-120 for box B. Finally, the computer compares the RGB values of the pixel in A and the pixel in B, identifies a match, and concludes that box A and box B are the exact same color. The results are clear to the computer.

So which is it? After taking into consideration the results from the computer algorithm, would you still consider A darker than B? We don't know about you, but we still think A looks darker than B—call us crazy. But then that's what makes us human—we aren't perfect.

The sad reality is the computer is correct, and our perception is wrong. Our mind is being fooled by an illusion created by a vision scientist at MIT, Professor Ed Adelson. Dr. Adelson exploits local contrast between neighboring checker squares, and the mind's perception of the pillar as casting a shadow. The combination creates a powerful illusion that tricks every human mind. The human mind is, as succinctly stated by Duke Psychology Professor Dan Ariely, "predictably irrational."

That may seem to be a strong statement. Perhaps the illusion as revealed in Figure 1.2 has convinced you that our minds may not be perfect in certain isolated settings (yes, the parallel bars are the same color from top to bottom). Or perhaps it has only persuaded you to believe that while a subset of the population may be flawed, you still possess a perfectly rational and

Edward H. Adelson

FIGURE 1.2 Ed Adelson Checkerboard Illusion Answer

logical mind. Don't be too sure, as a well-established body of academic literature in psychology demonstrates conclusively that humans are prone to poor decision-making across a broad range of situations.

But what about experts? Surely, experts are beyond the grip of such cognitive bias? We often assume that professionals with years of experience and expertise in a particular field are better equipped and incentivized to make unbiased decisions. Unfortunately for experts, and for those who rely on them, the academic evidence is unequivocal: systematic decision-making, which relies on models, outperforms discretionary decision-making, or experts. We will come back to this point in a moment, but first let's discuss some other reasons experts might not always provide flawless advice.

WHAT ARE THE EXPERTS' INCENTIVES?

When paying a financial expert to manage your money, a good question to ask is the following: What are the experts' incentives? This is important to know, because even if the expert has true knowledge about financial markets, misaligned incentives can destroy an *edge* the expert has, or make the expert look better than he really is. Here are a few examples of when experts' incentives might not be properly aligned:

- *Focusing on short-term vs. long-term results.* Consider a financial expert creating a value strategy with an assumed "edge," or ability to beat the market in the long run. This expert can decide to invest in 200 of her best stock ideas or 50 of her best stock ideas. The expert faces a trade-off between these two approaches. On one hand, the expert knows that, over the long-haul, buying the cheapest 50 value stocks will be a better risk-adjusted bet than the 200-stock portfolio, since the larger portfolio would be dilutive to performance in the long run. On the other hand, the expert also understands that the 50-stock portfolio has a higher chance of losing to a standard benchmark in a given year, which will could cause her to lose clients in that year. The expert, who assumes, correctly, that most investors focus on short-term results, will opt for a 200-stock portfolio in order to minimize downside risk (and retain clients), and thus, will create a suboptimal product that doesn't fully leverage her expertise. In effect, the expert is indeed an expert, but there is an incentive alignment problem between the expert and investors that negates the benefits of her expertise.

■ *Exploiting authority to generate business.* Let's say we have two financial experts. One expert shows up in a pair of jeans and a sweatshirt and states that simply investing in the S&P 500 from 1927 to 2013 has a return of 9.91 percent on average. The second expert shows up in an Armani suit, with his research team of PhDs (also in suits) behind him, and tells you that with his investment technique, $100 would have grown to $371,452 from 1927 to 2013. "*Wow,*" you would say, and then ask, "So what are the details of the strategy?" Our straight-talking sweatshirt and jeans expert might say, "Well, you simply buy and hold the S&P 500 Index and reinvest dividends to achieve the 9.91 percent return." However, our Armani-suited PhD squad may respond with the following: "Our strategy is proprietary, is built off of 30 years of research by 15 PhDs, and seeks to dynamically allocate to certain sectors of the market, with more weight going toward better-performing securities." Sounds impressive, but the strategy is the same: Buy and hold the market! Sadly, that is the expert's power over the layman. If you are unable to fully interpret the advice of an expert, you may be beguiled by his overblown rhetoric masquerading as skill. Overall, an investor needs to be aware of experts' incentives to leverage their position of authority. If an expert cannot explain his strategy to you in a simple, understandable way, we recommend walking in the other direction.

■ *Favoring complexity over simplicity.* All else equal, a financial expert prefers a more complex model to a simple one. Why? Because complex models allow them to charge higher fees! As we will show later in the book, simple models beat complex models, and they certainly beat human experts. Why would an expert, many of whom are informed of this fact, recommend a complex solution other than for an increased fee? Consider two asset-allocation alternatives: The first option is an "optimized, time-varying, strategic allocation approach, based on years of research," whereas, the second option is a 50/50 split between stocks and bonds, buy and hold forever. Also consider that both approaches sell for a 1 percent management fee and you have to choose one of the options. Your instinct probably suggests the more advanced version. But why? What if the simpler option is actually superior to the more complex one?

Overall, there are some true experts in the field. We recommend focusing on those experts who have long-term goals, are transparent about their investment strategy, and have an ability to explain their approach in one sentence.

ARE EXPERTS WORTHLESS?

To be clear: We are not making the claim that human experts are worthless across all aspects of the decision-making process. Dentists are great at filling cavities, surgeons are quite handy at repairing ACLs, and the right financial advisor can protect us from making expensive mistakes. Experts are critical, but only for certain elements of the decision-making process. To better frame the decision-making problem, we break the decision-making process into three components (see Figure 1.3):

- Research and development (build systems)
- Systematic implementation (implement systems)
- Evidence-based assessment (assess systems)

We would argue that human experts are required for the first and third phases of a decision-making process, which are the research and development phase and the assessment phase, respectively. The crux of our argument is that human experts should not be involved in the second phase of decision-making, or the implementation phase.

During the research and development phase of decision-making, experts build and test new ideas. In this phase, experts are required to create a sensible model. In the second phase—implementation—one should eliminate human involvement and rely on systematic execution. Finally, during the assessment phase of decision-making, one should once again rely on human experts to analyze and assess model performance to make improvements and incorporate lessons learned from the implementation phase.

We look to the real world for insights into how this three-phase decision-making framework might be applied in practice. A great case study

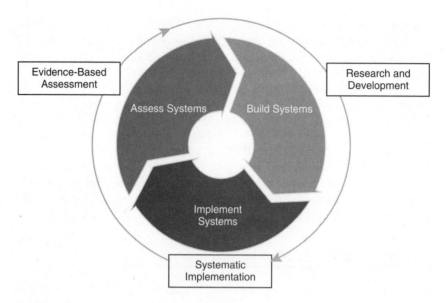

FIGURE 1.3   The Decision-Making Process

exists within the US Marine Corps (USMC), where Wes spent nearly four years as an officer deployed in a variety of combat situations. The USMC relies on "standard operating procedures," or SOPs, particularly when Marines are in harm's way. SOPs are developed according to the three-step process mentioned above, which is designed to establish the most robust, effective, and systematic decision-making process possible.

One example is the SOP for setting up a defensive position in a combat situation.[7] In the first phase of SOP development, experienced combat veterans and expert consultants review past data and lessons from the field to develop a set of rules that Marines will follow when establishing a defensive position. These rules are debated and agreed upon in an environment that emphasizes slow, deliberate, and critical thought. The current rules, or SOP, for a defensive position is summarized by the acronym SAFE:

- Security
- Automatic weapons on avenues of approach
- Fields of fire
- Entrenchment

During the second phase—the implementation phase—of SAFE, Marines in combat are directed to "follow the model," or adhere to the SOP. The last thing a Marine should do is disregard SOPs in the middle of a firefight, when the environment is chaotic, Marines are tired, and human decisions are most prone to error. Marines are trained from the beginning to avoid "comfort-based" decisions and to follow standard operating procedures. Of course, once the battle is over, Marines in the field will conduct a debrief and send this information back to the experts, who can debate and assess in a calm environment whether the current SOP needs to be changed based on empirical experience gleaned from the field—the third phase. A key principle of this three-step decision-making process is that discretionary experts are required to develop and assess, but execution is made systematic, so as to minimize human error. The Marines, like other critical decision makers, want experts to develop and assess SOPs in a stable training environment. However, the Marines want to implement SOPs systematically when the environment shifts from the training environment to the live battlefield.

THE EXPERT'S HYPOTHESIS

The so-called *expert's hypothesis,* which asserts that experts can outperform models, is intuitive and tells a deceptively compelling story. For example, to most, it seems like common sense that a hedge fund manager with a Harvard MBA and 20 years of work experience at Goldman Sachs can beat a simple model that buys a basket of low P/E stocks. The logic behind this presumption is persuasive, as the expert would seem to possess a number of advantages over the model. The expert can arguably outperform the simple model for the following reasons:

- Experts have access to qualitative information.
- Experts have more data.
- Experts have intuition and experience.

Of course, there are other ways to support the argument that a human expert will beat a simple model, but most of these stories revolve around the same key points already outlined.

The following three arguments, however, underlie the expert's hypothesis, and while they are plausible, they are wrong:

1. Qualitative information increases forecast accuracy.
2. More information increases forecast accuracy.
3. Experience and intuition enhance forecast accuracy.

Remarkably, the evidence we will present illustrates that qualitative information, more information, and experience/intuition do not lead to more accurate or reliable forecasts, but instead lead to poorer decision-making. And because this result is so counterintuitive, it makes it that much more important to understand.

Among the hundreds of cases of expert forecasts gone awry, one high-profile example is Meredith Whitney.[8] Ms. Whitney is famous for her prescient forecast of the banking crisis that reared its ugly head in late 2008. Public accounts of Ms. Whitney's predictions which were widely observed and discussed during that time period, all suggested that Ms. Whitney was a "genius" after her remarkable call on Citibank's balance sheet blues.

But Ms. Whitney didn't stop there. She outlined her gloomy forecast for the municipal bond market on a December 2010 segment of the prime-time CBS news program *60 Minutes*. Ms. Whitney predicted there would be "50 to 100 sizable defaults." She forcefully reiterated her prediction at the Spring 2012 Grant's Interest Rate Observer Conference, where we observed firsthand the emotional conviction Ms. Whitney felt for her bold prediction.

However, Ms. Whitney's powers of prediction were fleeting. In an article published in September 2012, the *Wall Street Journal* published a stinging article titled "Meredith Whitney Blew a Call—And Then Some." The piece was quick to point out that that "there were just five defaults" in the municipal market.[9]

Ms. Whitney was off by at least a factor of 10.

Whitney's missed call embodies the assumptions underlying the expert hypothesis. She was a well-known expert with access to the best qualitative and quantitative data available. That, coupled with her well-known previous experience and astute intuition, made her story compelling to the media and other experts alike. Many believed that Whitney simply had to be right. Whitney, like everyone else, also thought she had to be right. She had access to important people in local and state governments who provided her with privileged "soft" information; she studied thousands of pages of municipal-bond term-sheets and macroeconomic research reports; and her recent experience making the call on the financial crisis crystallized in her own mind that she could trust her "gut." Unfortunately, the potent combination of realized success and intense effort, gives human experts the "illusion of skill,"[10] which translates into overconfidence and a failure to appreciate randomness. In other words, our highest conviction decisions are apt to cause us the most problems.

SUMMARY

In this chapter, we described how a supposed expert, Victor Niederhoffer, twice blew up his funds through his hubris. We also described how this should make us all question our own expertise, since, like Niederhoffer, we too are flawed and irrational in predictable ways. Indeed, it makes sense to question essentially all experts, and to focus especially on their incentives, since we so often trust experts with critical decision-making. In fact, we should never trust experts to make on-the-fly decisions, although we should rely on them for their ability to develop and evaluate a systematic process. Finally, we examined the expert's hypothesis, which refers to the notion that human experts will outperform decision-making models. It is natural to believe in the superiority of expert judgment, which compels most to believe the expert's hypothesis. But experts can also be spectacularly wrong, as with Meredith Whitney, who was unable to follow up her Citibank call with another accurate judgment on the municipal bond market. In the next chapter, we'll more carefully investigate how experts and models compare.

NOTES

1. Mick Winstein, "Victor Niederhoffer after He Lost Everything in the 1997 Asian Crisis," *Smarter Investing* (June 3, 2013), http://investing.covestor.com/2013/06/victor-niederhoffer-after-he-lost-everything-in-the-1997-asian-crisis-video.
2. John Cassidy, "The Blow-Up Artist," *New Yorker Magazine* (October 15, 2007).
3. Bill Ziemba, "Hedge Fund Risk, Disasters and Their Prevention," *Wilmott* magazine (June 2, 2006), http://www.wilmott.com/pdfs/060206_drz.pdf.
4. R. Ziemba and W. Ziemba, *Scenarios for Risk Management and Global Investment Strategies* (New York: John Wiley & Sons, 2007).
5. "Mathematics Common Sense and Good Luck: My Life and Careers," MIT Video (December 9, 2010), http://video.mit.edu/watch/mathematics-common-sense-and-good-luck-my-life-and-careers-9644/.
6. Edward Adelson, "Checkershadow Illusion," accessed February 10, 2014, http://persci.mit.edu/gallery/checkershadow.
7. Marine Rifle Squad, MCRP 3-11.2, Chapter 5.
8. We do not mean to single out Meredith Whitney. The same point can be made with just about any analyst who has shown up on CBNC and expressed a confident and detailed opinion on a forecast.
9. David Weidner, "Meredith Whitney Blew a Call—And Then Some," *Wall Street Journal* (September 27, 2012), http://online.wsj.com/news/articles/SB10000872396390444549204578021380172883800.
10. Daniel Kahneman, *Thinking, Fast and Slow* (New York: Macmillan, 2012), p. 212.

CHAPTER 2

Simple Models Typically Beat the Experts

"We have to tell Jon that enough is enough. We need to take the keys away from him."
—The Treasurer of MF Global's parent company[1]

Several years ago, David had been reading a lot of investing books and decided that he wanted to experiment with some strategies he thought looked promising. David, armed with a Wharton MBA and over 20 years as a financial professional, felt he could make some money in the commodities and futures markets. He familiarized himself with the workings of the futures markets, and established a trading account at MF Global, a major commodity futures and derivatives broker.

When David transferred a block of capital to MF Global and began trading, he was relying on the expertise of the firm's CEO, Jon Corzine, to ensure the firm could execute trades and clear transactions, carefully maintain the segregation of customer accounts from proprietary brokerage funds, and perhaps most important of all, keep the firm solvent. David assumed he had nothing to fear with Corzine running the firm, since Corzine—a Goldman Sachs wunderkind and ultra-sophisticated bond trader—was just the kind of financial expert you would want at the helm.

David was therefore stunned when MF Global declared bankruptcy in late 2011. Then, a short time later, came another surprising development: the bankruptcy trustee announced that a $1.2 billion shortfall had been discovered in customer accounts. David wanted his capital returned, but no one seemed to know where it was. How could this have occurred under Jon Corzine's watch?

Previously, it seemed Jon Corzine could do no wrong. He produced powerful financial insights for Goldman Sachs, generated huge bond trading profits, and had effortlessly charted a remarkable professional path. Indeed, things had always seemed to come easily to Jon Corzine. While in high school, he was the quarterback of the football team and captain of the basketball team. In addition to being athletic, he was also academically talented; in 1969, he graduated Phi Beta Kappa from the University of Illinois at Urbana-Champaign. He was a go-getter, and a man of diverse talents, simultaneously serving in the US Marine Corps Reserve, and pursuing an MBA at the University of Chicago at night, and subsequently getting his feet wet in the financial industry working in the bond departments of several banks. He had financial aptitude and was a clear up-and-comer. For someone for whom things seemed to come so easily, it was only natural that he eventually landed as a bond trader for Goldman Sachs, one of the most well-known and respected investment banks on Wall Street. But, at that point, things really began to go well for him.

Corzine advanced swiftly through the ranks at Goldman, making partner after a few short years, and becoming co-head of fixed income. He was one of a few early architects of Goldman's aggressive push into the bond trading business, and into Asia, both hugely profitable strategies that allowed Goldman to morph from an investment bank into a trading powerhouse that, in some ways, resembled an immense hedge fund. Corzine continued his meteoric rise, eventually becoming CEO and chairman of the firm, which some might consider to be the zenith of achievement on Wall Street. Corzine was the head banker in a firm full of bankers. Clearly, he had achieved a degree of expertise that was rare in the industry, and had even done so within one of the most competitive firms on Wall Street. Corzine capped his experience at Goldman with a stint as a US senator representing New Jersey, and was also elected as its governor. Clearly, Corzine had leadership skills and sound judgment.

So what on earth happened at MF Global? Was Corzine, the consummate Wall Street insider and expert, somehow to blame? Had he miscalculated in some way? In order to understand what went wrong at MF Global, which was essentially brought down by a bad bond trade, it's necessary to review how securities dealers are financed using the so-called "repo" market, which refers to a type of financing involving repurchase agreements. In a repo transaction, one party sells an asset to a second party at one price, while agreeing to repurchase or "repo" the assets from the second party at another price in the future. If the first party fails to repurchase the securities, the second party then owns the assets. The repo market, sometimes referred to as the *shadow banking system,* has exploded over the past decade, with some estimating that its size may exceed that for the entire US banking system. In essence, the repo market has become the lifeblood of the financial system.

So how does the repo financing technique relate to MF Global's situation?

Jon Corzine, as an expert bond trader, understood the financing power inherent in the repo market, and saw it as a funding mechanism that would allow MF Global to enhance corporate profits by expressing his view on the outcomes of specific bond transactions. And during 2011, in Corzine's expert opinion, there was money to be made in European bonds.

MF Global bought a lot of European bonds, and then in a chain of repo transactions used them as collateral for new loans, using the cash proceeds from these to buy yet more European bonds. In Corzine's view, the transaction wasn't risky in the sense that the firm had exposure to default risk—the European Financial Stability Facility guaranteed them—and Corzine had also engineered the bond transactions to include a repurchase obligation that occurred at the same time the bonds matured, in a so-called *repo-to-maturity* transaction. Corzine's bond transactions looked to be low risk, with a large guaranteed profit built in when the bonds were repurchased. In a sense, MF Global had become a kind of institutional-scale hedge fund, directed by Jon Corzine, and it was making a leveraged bond bet.

MF Global was, however, exposed to the risks involved in maintaining the trade itself. While the spread (price paid versus price received upon repurchase) was hugely profitable, there was the risk of margin calls and other frictional costs. If the bonds decreased in value, MF Global might have to post additional collateral to maintain its leveraged positions. At its peak, MF Global's leverage reached a reported 40-to-1 ratio. As the European sovereign debt crisis grew, FINRA required MF Global to post more and more collateral. The costs to maintain the trade quickly swamped the firm's capital base and MF Global met its steamroller.

When MF Global got overleveraged in its big repo bet, the firm's counterparties merely did what any good capitalist does when a borrower defaults: they exercised their right to take possession of the collateral on the loan. But the problem for David was that in the chaos of the collateral call the assets in his margin account became entangled with other MF Global collateral, and when the dust settled, some big institution was holding onto his cash. It took years before his capital was returned.

So was Corzine an expert? Well, yes, he was in the sense that he knew a lot about bond trading and bond markets, and how to run a proprietary bond trading business for Goldman Sachs. But he wasn't an expert in the sense that as the CEO of MF Global, he bankrupted it by entering into an overleveraged repo bond trade. Arguably, by definition, financial experts aren't supposed to bankrupt their firms.

As with the earlier case of Victor Niederhoffer, who bankrupted one fund, and nearly bankrupted a second fund, we again see how relying on someone who is supposedly an expert can lead to an outcome that is simply not supposed to happen when an expert is in charge.

THE EVIDENCE SHOWS . . .[2]

As we discussed in the last chapter, the expert's hypothesis states that human experts can beat simple models. To substantiate the argument that the expert's hypothesis is false, we stand on the shoulders of academic researchers, who have studied this hypothesis for over half a century.

To give readers a flavor for how academic research has studied the relative performance of models versus experts, we introduce a study on parole recidivism predictions.[3] The study was facilitated by a partnership between a group of academic researchers and the Pennsylvania Board of Probation and Parole to identify ways to make the parole process more accurate, fair, and cost-effective. Professor Carroll and his team set up the experiment as follows:

- *Experts Parole Board:* Equip human parole officers with information to make parole board decisions based on quantitative and qualitative information. This information included interviews with parolees, interviews with people known by the parolee, information on past criminal history, demographics, and so forth.
- *Model Parole Board:* Create a simple predictive model based on simple factors. The baseline model is focused on three areas: offense type; number of past convictions; and number of prison rule violations.

The researchers compared the performance of the "experts" versus the simple model. The summary finding is that a simple model, while far from perfect, is over *three times* more effective than experts at forecasting recidivism (see Figure 2.1).

The research results were not lost on practitioners in the real world. A 2013 *Wall Street Journal* article, "State Parole Boards Use Software to Decide Which Inmates to Release,"[4] highlights how algorithmic parole decisions are now the norm, and no longer the exception.

The article describes how, under budgetary pressures, many states have begun using computerized risk assessments to reduce rates of recidivism, and thus overall incarceration rates. For example, Michigan introduced computerized assessments in 2006, and by 2008 had reduced its three-year recidivism rate by 10 percent, and significantly reduced the overall prison population.

So an early recidivism study seemed to indicate that models beat experts, and when deployed in the real world computerized assessments have lowered recidivism. Why do the models beat the experts in predicting recidivism?

The judgments of human parole boards can be affected by human emotion and perception, and can be based on intuition or subjective criteria, with

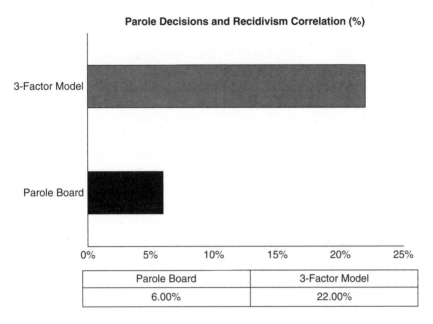

Parole Decisions and Recidivism Correlation (%)

Parole Board	3-Factor Model
6.00%	22.00%

FIGURE 2.1 Parole Decisions and Recidivism Correlation

humans focusing on the wrong factors. For instance, human parole boards rely on considerations such as an interview with the offender and whether an offender shows remorse as predictors of future recidivism. But are these the right factors to be emphasizing? Or do parole boards assume these "soft" elements matter, without examining the evidence? Risk assessment models, which are based on research by criminologists, suggest that more subtle, alternative factors, such as age of first arrest, and whether an offender believes his conviction is unfair may be far better indicators of the likelihood of recidivism. Although these signals are statistically strong predictors, they sometimes directly conflict with human intuition.

A STUDY OF ALL THE STUDIES

Thus far, we've presented a formal study relating to how models beat experts in the domain of recidivism, and how computerized assessments seem to be making a difference in the real world, and described some of the behavioral reasons why this appears to be the case.

In order to make a more convincing case that models beat experts, we require more analysis. Professors William Grove, David Zald, Boyd Lebow, Beth Snitz, and Chad Nelson have performed a meta-analysis—or a study of studies—on 136 published studies that analyze the accuracy of "actuarial" (i.e., computers/models) versus "clinical" (i.e., human experts) judgment.[5]

The studies examined by Grove et al. include forecast accuracy estimates that cut across a huge variety of professions. The studies included examples from the following fields:

- College academic performance
- Magazine advertising sales
- Success in military training
- Diagnosis of appendicitis
- Business failure
- Suicide attempts
- University admissions
- Marital satisfaction
- Wine quality

The study's results are stunning: Models beat experts 46 percent of the time; models equal or beat experts 94 percent of the time; and experts beat models a mere 6 percent of the time (see Figure 2.2). The empirical

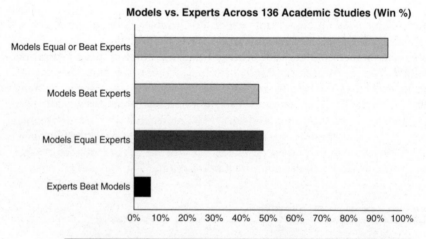

Experts Beat Models	Models Equal Experts	Model Beat Experts	Model Equal or Beat Experts
5.88%	47.79%	46.32%	94.12%

FIGURE 2.2 Models vs. Experts Across 136 Academic Studies (Win %)

evidence that systematic decision processes meet or exceed discretionary decision-making would seem to be overwhelming. The executive summary of the study states it succinctly: *Superiority for mechanical-prediction techniques was consistent, regardless of the judgment task, type of judges, judges' amounts of experience, or the types of data being combined.* —*Grove et al.*[6]

The empirical evidence on the horse race between model-driven decisions and discretionary decision-making is clear, maybe even a slam dunk, but the implications are unsettling. How is it possible that a simple algorithm can consistently beat expert opinion? The answer to this conundrum lies with cognitive bias, which we will return to in a moment. But first, let's consider an important question that naturally relates to these results.

WHAT IF EXPERTS HAVE THE MODEL?

Although evidence clearly suggests that models meet—and often beat—experts across a variety of contexts, scholars were also inspired to tackle another question: *How do experts perform if they are given the results of the model?*

Dano Leli and Susan Filskov explore this question in their 1984 study, "Clinical Detection of Intellectual Deterioration Associated with Brain Damage." The study's premise is simple, and begins in the traditional way, by pitting models against experts. First, place experienced psychologists and a simple prediction algorithm head-to-head in a horse race, and determine which can more accurately classify the extent of a patient's brain impairment. As before, the model utilizes a systematic approach based on a statistical model of prior data; meanwhile, the humans can utilize their vast expertise and intuition based on years of experience.

The results from the study should be, by now, somewhat expected, yet they are still striking. The simple quantitative model has a classification accuracy ratio of 83.3 percent, which was much higher than for the experienced clinicians, who had a success rate of only 58.3 percent. Interestingly, the inexperienced clinicians were slightly better at 62.5 percent. As we saw previously, the model (and the novices) clearly beat the experts.

But this time the researchers took their analysis one step further. They wanted to explore what would happen when the experts were armed with the powerful prediction model. A natural hypothesis is that experts, equipped with the model, would outperform the stand-alone model. In other words, models might represent a floor on performance, to which the experts could add performance.

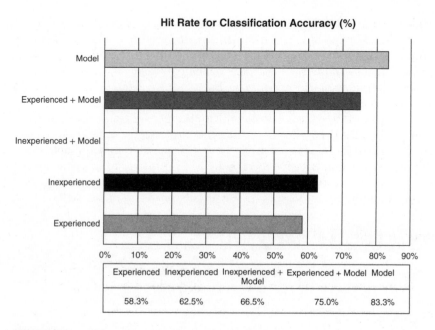

FIGURE 2.3 Hit Rate for Classification Accuracy (%)

In follow-on tests, the researchers gave the experts the output of the model and disclosed that the model had "previously demonstrated high predictive validity in identifying the presence or absence of intellectual deterioration associated with brain damage." Using the model, experienced clinicians significantly improved their accuracy ratio from 58.3 percent to 75 percent and the inexperienced clinicians moved from 62.5 percent to 66.5 percent. Nonetheless, the experts were still unable to outperform the stand-alone model, which had already established the gold standard 83.3 percent success rate. This study suggests that models don't represent a floor on performance; rather, models reflect a ceiling on performance, from which the experts detract performance. The "secret sauce" of human judgment ruins the beautiful simplicity and effectiveness of a mechanistic calculation (see Figure 2.3).

BUT INVESTING IS DIFFERENT, RIGHT?

But surely these results should not apply to the world of investing, where things must be different. Many investors think money managers are a special breed of human, and that a human financial expert, armed with a model, can generate outsized returns in financial markets—or in other words, financial models do not represent a ceiling on performance, but are a performance floor to which a human manager can add value. Carson Boneck, global head of investment management for S&P Capital IQ, captures this sentiment in a May 2013 interview: "We think quantamental is going to be a big theme driving our client portfolios and our own product strategy."[7]

Quantamental seeks to unite man and model, using the best of both. Mr. Boneck tells a great story: A discretionary stock-picking expert armed with a powerful model may create a powerful combination. But investment clients should ask if there is any evidence that a quantamental approach—a process that involves the use of models to screen for promising stocks, but overlays a human element to make the final investment decision—actually adds value.

One might argue that the experts in the Leli and Filskov (1984) study, from earlier, were sub par and perhaps the study design was flawed. Or perhaps these results are only relevant to the field of brain research. Expert stock pickers, by contrast, have years of experience in the investment management business and access to superior fundamental research tools, and they can develop a more pronounced qualitative information edge. Stock pickers can't possibly be beaten by simple models, can they? As it turns out, we have a reasonable real-world laboratory that provides insight into this question.

Joel Greenblatt, famous for his bestselling books *You Can Be a Stock Market Genius* and *The Little Book that Beats the Market*, stumbled into a natural experiment. Joel's firm, Formula Investing, utilizes a simple algorithm that buys firms that rank high on an average of their cheapness and their quality ranking. The firm offers investors separately managed accounts (SMAs) and investors have a choice in how to invest:

1. Invest using only the model's output.
2. Receive the model's output, but use their own discretion to identify stocks held in the portfolio.

Joel collected data on all their SMAs from May 2009 through April 2011 and tabulated the results. He wanted to know if adding discretion to the investment process would improve results (see Figure 2.4).

The automatic accounts earned a total return of 84.1 percent, besting the S&P 500 Index's 62.7 percent mark by over 20 percentage points.[8] The self-managed accounts, which allowed the clients to pick and choose from the model's output at their discretion, earned a respectable 59.4 percent. However, the 59.4 percent figure was worse than the passive benchmark, and much worse than the account performance for the automatic

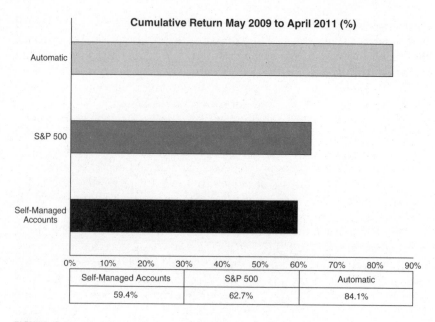

FIGURE 2.4 Cumulative Return May 2009 to April 2011 (%)

accounts.[9] The takeaway from this study is similar to the brain impairment research by Leli and Filskov: *Models represent a ceiling on performance, not a floor.*

WHY EXPERTS FAIL TO BEAT MODELS

Daniel Kahneman's magnum opus, *Thinking, Fast and Slow*,[10] describes how human intuition affects our decision-making. The thesis of the book is that humans are driven by two modes of thinking: System 1 and System 2.

- *System 1:* Decisions are instinctual and heuristic-based.
- *System 2:* Processes are calculated and analytical.

System 1 thinking, while imperfect, is speedy and highly efficient. For example, if Joe is facing the threat of a large tiger charging him at full speed, Joe's System 1 thinking will trigger him to turn around and sprint for the nearest tree, and ask questions later. As an alternative, Joe's System 2 thinking will calculate the speed of the tiger's approach and assess his situation. Joe will examine his options and realize that there is an armored vehicle a few steps away. On average, if Joe immediately sprints to the tree he may get lucky and outrun the tiger; on the other hand, if Joe stops, thinks through his tiger-escaping options, and rationally selects the optimal choice for escape, well, there may be one less Joe in the jungle ...

Joe's hypothetical situation highlights why evolution has created System 1; on average, running for the tree is a simple and reliable life-saving decision, versus the more complex and time-consuming alternative of thinking through the options and making a so-called "rational" decision. While System 1 is uber-efficient and fast, the downside of System 1 is that its "fight or flight" nature often leads to systematic bias: Joe will *always* run for the tree, even when the better decision may be to stop, think about alternatives, and jump in the armored vehicle.

System 1 certainly served its purpose when humans were faced with life and death situations in the jungles. In modern-day life, where saber-tooth tigers are less common and long-term consequences are the norm, the benefits of immediate decisions rarely outweigh the costs of flawed decision-making. In finance, the necessity of avoiding System 1 and relying on System 2 in the context of navigating financial markets is of utmost importance.

Below are three core reasons why human experts underperform systematic simple models, with each cause discussed in more detail in the following chapters.

1. Same Facts; Different Decisions

Humans, unlike models, can take the same set of facts and arrive at different conclusions. This can happen for a variety of reasons, but a lack of human consistency is often attributed to reacting to what you first hear (anchoring bias), reacting to your immediate environment (framing effects), or relying exclusively on information that is readily available (availability bias). We will return to these common biases later. A computer suffers from none of these ailments—same input, same output.

2. Overconfidence

Humans are consistently overconfident. Overconfidence can be driven by errors such as hindsight bias—believing past events were more predictable ex-ante than they actually were—and self-attribution bias—attributing good outcomes to skill and poor outcomes to bad luck. Systematic decisions limit these problems. Models don't get emotionally involved and don't have an ego. Therefore, they are unable to get overconfident or overoptimistic—they simply execute based on the facts.

3. Story-Based, Not Evidence-Based Decisions

Humans suffer from a proclivity to believe in stories, or explanations that fit a fact pattern, but they don't bother to fully consider the empirical evidence. For example, consider the following statement:

> *Linda is thirty-one years old, single, outspoken, and very bright. She majored in philosophy. As a student, she was deeply concerned with issues of discrimination and social justice, and also participated in antiwar demonstrations.*

Is it more likely that Linda is a bank teller or that Linda is a bank teller and is active in the non-GMO (genetically modified organisms) food movement? Our gut instinct is to think that it is more likely that Linda is a non-GMO bank teller, since the concepts of discrimination and social justice activate stored memories that are traditionally associated with environmental activism. But this line of reasoning is incorrect, as it ignores the statistical reality.[11] System 1's love for a coherent story has led us to make a poor judgment, which is divorced from the true underlying probabilities. An empirical-based decision would consider the fact that the bank teller population is much larger than the non-GMO bank teller population and immediately understand that it is statistically more likely that Linda is only a bank teller. We have been led astray by our urge to create a story in our heads that seems to describe the evidence.

SUMMARY

This chapter began with a description of Jon Corzine, an extremely experienced and accomplished financial expert, who managed to bankrupt a giant commodity brokerage firm. This anecdote gives rise to the notion that we should be skeptical of experts. To explore this question further, we reviewed the case of recidivism, and how models seem to beat experts both in a study as well as in the real world. Next, we reviewed a meta-study, which showed that models meet or beat experts across a variety of settings. We then highlighted additional research that showed experts couldn't beat a model, even when armed with output from the model. This also appears to be the case with investing, where clients systematically detracted from their portfolio's performance when they overrode the model's recommendation. Finally, we discussed why experts, who are influenced by their intuition, are often wrong.

Here's the bottom line: everyone makes mistakes. And because we recognize our frequent irrational urges, we often seek the judgment of experts, to avoid becoming our own worst enemy. We assume that experts, with years of experience in their particular fields, are better equipped and incentivized to make unbiased decisions. But is this assumption valid? A surprisingly robust, but neglected branch of academic literature, has studied, for more than 60 years, the assumption that experts make unbiased decisions. The evidence tells a decidedly one-sided story: Systematic decision-making, through the use of simple quantitative models with limited inputs, outperforms discretionary decisions made by experts. We'll leave the last word to Paul Meehl, the eminent scholar in the field of psychology, *"There is no controversy in social science that shows such a large body of qualitatively diverse studies coming out so uniformly in the same direction as this one [models outperform experts]."*[12]

NOTES

1. US Commodity Futures Trading Commission vs. MF Global Inc. Civil Action No. 4463 accessed December 29, 2014, http://www.cftc.gov/ucm/groups/public/ @lrenforcementactions/documents/legalpleading/enfmfglobalcomplaint062713 .pdf.
2. In the jargon of academia, the term for experts is *clinician* and the term for models is *actuarial process*. Instead of using "clinical versus actuarial," I use "models versus experts" to facilitate understanding within our chosen context.
3. J. Carroll, R. Wiener, J. Galegher, and J. Alibrio, "Evaluation, Diagnosis, and Prediction in Parole Decision-Making," *Law and Society Review* 17 (1982): 199–228.
4. Joseph Walker, "State Parole Boards Use Software to Decide Which Inmates to Release: Programs Look at Prisoners' Biographies for Patterns That Predict Future Crime," *Wall Street Journal* (October 11, 2013).
5. W. Grove, D. Zald, B. Lebow, and B. Nelson, "Clinical Versus Mechanical Prediction: A Meta-Analysis," *Psychological Assessment* 12 (2000): 19–30.
6. Ibid.
7. Carson Boneck, "S&P Capital IQ: Views on Alpha Ideas for Global Equity Markets," *S&P Capital IQ* (May 28, 2013), accessed February 10, 2014, http://www.youtube.com/watch?v=tThxb_eFUTo.
8. Joel Greenblatt, "Adding Your Two Cents May Cost a Lot over the Long Term." Perspectives, *Morningstar,* January 16, 2012; http://news.morningstar.com/ articlenet/SubmissionsArticle.aspx?submissionid=134195.xml&part=2
9. J. Greenblatt, "Adding Your Two Cents May Cost You a Lot Over the Long-Term," *Morningstar* (2011).
10. Daniel Kahneman, *Thinking, Fast and Slow* (New York: Macmillan, 2012).

11. Assume there are 200 females, 100 female bank tellers, and 50 female feminists in the world. It is more likely that Linda is a bank teller ($100/200 = 50\%$) because the subset of bank tellers that are also feminist (best case is that all feminists are bank tellers implies $50/200 = 25\%$) is much smaller than the population of bank tellers as a group (100).
12. Paul Meehl, "Causes and Effects of My Disturbing Little Book," *Journal of Personality Assessment* 50 (1986): 370–375.

CHAPTER 3

Experts Are Biased and Overconfident

"How were you feeling when you got out of bed thirteen years ago, when you're looking at historical simulations? Did you like what the model said, or did you not like what the model said? It's a hard thing to back-test."

—Jim Simons, CEO, Renaissance Technologies, LLC

While stationed in Iraq, Wes saw stunning displays of poor decision-making. Obviously, in areas where violence could break out at any moment, it was of paramount importance to stay focused on standard operating procedures, or SOPs. But, in extreme conditions where temperatures regularly reached over 125 degrees, stressed and sleep-deprived humans can sometimes do irrational things.

For example, carrying 80 pounds of gear in the frying desert sun makes you hot and uncomfortable. But many things that are necessary for survival in a combat environment, such as extra water, ammunition, and protective gear, are heavy and bulky. A completely rational thinker weighs the cost of carrying gear (profuse sweat, physical discomfort, and so forth) against the benefits (a better chance of not dying). A more emotionally driven decision maker disregards a cost/benefit analysis and goes with his natural instinct—toss all the gear, get some fresh air, hope for the best, and statistical likelihood of death be damned. An example of a rational approach to combat and an irrational approach to combat are highlighted in Figure 3.1.

In Figure 3.1, Wes is situated at a combat checkpoint in Haditha, a village in Al Anbar Province of Iraq. Wes is explaining to his Iraqi counterparts

FIGURE 3.1   Rational and Irrational Behavior

how to set up a tactical checkpoint. A quick inspection of the photograph highlights how a stressful environment can make some people do irrational things. Wes and his Iraqi friend to his right in the photo are wearing their Kevlar helmets, carrying extra ammunition, and have a water source on their gear. The Kevlar is important because mortar rounds are periodically inbound. Rational reaction: Wear Kevlar to prevent hot metal fragments from entering one's head! The ammunition is important because one needs ammunition in a gunfight. Rational reaction: Carry ammo! Finally, water is important, because in 125-degree weather, a lack of hydration can lead to heat stroke. Rational reaction: Carry water! And while all of these things sound rational, the Iraqi on the far right isn't wearing a Kevlar, isn't carrying extra ammo, and doesn't have a source of water.

Is our irrational Iraqi friend abnormal? Not really. All human beings suffer from behavioral bias and these biases are magnified in stressful situations. After all, we're only human.

The conditions we describe in Iraq are analogous to conditions investors find in the markets. Watching our hard-earned wealth fluctuate in value is stressful—and although it is not as stressful as being in a war, it is still emotionally taxing. Stressful situations breed bad decisions. To minimize bad decisions in stressful environments, we need to deploy systematic decision-making.

The Marine Corps solution to bad decision-making involves a plethora of checklists and SOPs, as discussed earlier. To ensure these processes are followed, the Corps is religious about repetitive training. The Marines want to "de-program" our gut-instincts and re-program each Marine to "follow the model." And while this might sound a bit Orwellian, automated reactions in chaotic situations give us the best chance of survival. In combat, something as simple as a dead battery in a radio, or a forgotten map, can be the difference between life and death. To make good decisions in stressful situations, Marines follow a rigorous model that has been systematically developed and combat-proven. The lesson seems to be clear: in order for decision-making to be effective, it must be systematic. But to understand why systematic decision-making is important, we must first understand why ad-hoc decision-making is flawed.

THE BIASED BRAIN

Humans are not wired to engage in detailed cost/benefit analysis decision-making all of the time. It is too cognitively demanding. Natural selection has blessed—and cursed—us with efficient decision-making shortcuts known as heuristics. There are many heuristics our minds use to keep us working in our day-to-day lives. We highlight some of the more important heuristics and how they can lead to flawed decision-making in the context of financial markets. We cover the following in this chapter:

- Anchoring
- Framing
- Availability
- Physical state
- Overconfidence

Anchoring

Stimuli from the environment affect our discretionary decisions subconsciously. Oftentimes, we don't even know we are vulnerable to these subconscious actors on our conscious decisions. One important example is anchoring. Broadly defined, anchoring describes our tendency to rely too heavily, or *anchor,* on irrelevant information when making decisions.

An example comes from research by Professors Simonson and Drolet, who study how consumer behavior is affected by irrelevant anchors

AN EXAMPLE OF THE WILLINGNESS TO PAY WITH VALUE UNCERTAINTY TASK

Description: *Black & Decker Cooltouch Two-Slice <u>Toaster</u>.* Has super-wide slots for extra thick bread, bagels, and English muffins. Exterior stays cool to the touch. Removable crumb tray for easing cleaning.

First, please enter the last two digits of your social security number (SSN:)_____

1. Assume you are not sure if you want to buy the toaster, and if so, what price would you be willing to pay for it? Assume now that the last two digits of your SSN are a price in dollars. Would you be willing to buy this toaster at this price?   **YES/NO**
2. What is the lowest price for which you would be willing to buy this toaster/ $_____

FIGURE 3.2   Anchoring Example

(Figure 3.2).[1] The researchers ask buyers to assess their willingness to pay for a variety of products, to include a Black & Decker toaster. The setup is simple. Group A is asked how much they are willing to pay for a toaster. Group B is asked the same question; however, the researchers play a sinister trick on these hapless consumers. The Group B buyers are asked to write down the last two digits of their social security number (SSN) *prior* to asking the question about willingness to pay. The anchoring hypothesis predicts that buyers with higher SSN values will be willing to pay a higher amount and those with lower SSN will be willing to pay a lower amount.

Remarkably, the value for the last two digits of one's social security number *actually influences the buyer's willingness to pay.* Buyers with SSNs above 50 report a willingness to pay $32.50, whereas, buyers with SSNs less than 50 report being willing to pay $25. Those in the control group, who were not asked their SSN in advance, reported being willing to pay an average price of $30. The researchers repeat this experiment on different consumer products (phones, backpacks, headphones, etc.) and find similar results. The evidence from this study—and many similar studies—highlight the power of anchoring on our decision-making process (see Figure 3.3).

Marketing departments and retailers around the world are aware of this powerful effect and deploy it against us every day. Think about the last time you went to the store and found an item "on sale." "Wow!" you might think, "I can get this $80 shirt for 40 percent off!" The dramatic discount and the high price anchor triggers an emotional response, which make us

	WTP with SSN	
Last two digits of SSN	<50	>50
Product		
Toaster	$25	$32.5
Phone	50	70
Backpack	25	30
Radio Headphone	20	30
Average	*$30*	*$41*

FIGURE 3.3 Anchoring Example Results

more likely to buy the shirt! The same tactic is used by real estate brokers, car salesmen, and teenagers every day. The original purchase price acts as an "anchor," which subliminally impacts our "rational" minds and nudges us toward making a purchase.

But how might anchoring affect a professional stock-picking portfolio manager? Imagine the manager is conducting a discounted cash-flow analysis to determine a "buy" or "sell" recommendation. Her model requires an entry for what she believes to be the company's 10-year revenue growth forecast. Immediately before she enters in her assumption, two scenarios play out:

1. The manager's assistant walks in and mentions that her prior meeting with a new client has been moved to the *5th of January*.
2. The assistant walks in and mentions that her prior meeting with a new client has been moved to the *30th of January*.

The only difference in the two scenarios is the mention of "5th" and "30th." Is the manager going to enter the same revenue growth projection in both these scenarios? If Professor Kahneman's description of the strength of the anchoring bias is accurate, it is likely she will enter a higher growth rate number in the "30th" scenario:

"[Anchoring is] one of the most reliable and robust results of experimental psychology."[2]

Anchoring suggests that the portfolio manager will enter different growth forecasts into the model in these separate scenarios. The scariest part is that the manager won't even know this subliminal nudge is occurring, because anchoring effects are influencing the decision-making process subconsciously.

Scary stuff.

Framing

Framing is another bias that creeps into our minds behind the scenes and influences our behavior. The framing bias occurs because different ways of presenting information can evoke different emotions or alter our perceptions, which then leads to different decisions.

Consider the two middle circles in Figure 3.4.[3] Even though the middle circles are the same size, it appears that the circle on the right is larger than the one on the left because of framing. The right circle is surrounded by smaller circles, causing our brains to perceive the right circle as being large when compared with the surrounding smaller circles. However, the left circle is surrounded by larger circles, leading our brain to interpret it as being relatively smaller than the right circle. Go ahead, stare at the circles as long as you'd like. Our brains are programmed to perceive the two circles differently, based on the context, or frames, even though they are exactly the same size.

Amos Tversky and his colleagues study framing by changing how questions are asked.[4] They find that the same information can be conveyed using two different frames and people will respond in completely different ways, depending on which frame is used.

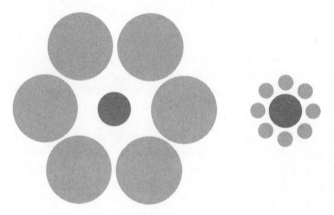

FIGURE 3.4   Framing Effect

We highlight a few representative examples below:
Do you prefer ground beef that is:

- *75 percent lean?*
- *25 percent fat?*

Who would ever want "fat" beef? Most people will choose ground beef that is 75 percent lean over 25 percent fat, without recognizing that the questions are exactly the same.

Another example:
Do you prefer a medication that has a:

- *90 percent chance of keeping you alive?*
- *10 percent chance of killing you?*

Our brains immediately think, "Staying alive or dying?—that's an easy question. I choose staying alive." Of course, we have to strain a bit to realize that the two propositions are exactly the same.

One doesn't have to think too hard to see how a financial advisor with training in psychology could influence her customers. Consider once again the financial advisor we discussed earlier, who tells her client the following:

"Stocks are better for the long run because they earned 9.91 percent a year from 1927 through 2013."

Take that same financial advisor, but have her frame the information a bit differently:

"Stocks are better for the long run because they grew $100 into $371,452 from 1927 through 2013."

This same advisor frames the information in a chart, shown in Figure 3.5.

Although the advisor technically offered the exact same information (stocks grew at 9.91 percent from 1927 to 2013), the framing of the second statement, alongside a fancy chart that enhances the framing effect, might encourage a client to allocate more to stocks. The thought of turning $100 into $371,452 is much more appealing at first glance than earning a comparatively "measly" 9.91 percent a year, which is an abstraction with less immediately perceived value. We are poor natural statisticians, and interpreting geometric growth rates is not intuitive to the human mind.

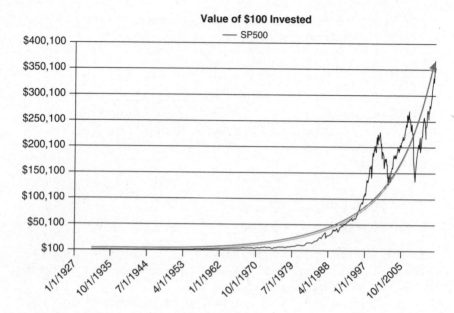

FIGURE 3.5   Value of $100 Invested

Availability Bias

Availability bias is an artifact of System 1, which causes our mind to overemphasize the importance of recent or easily recalled information. An applied example: Imagine that someone asks you whether there are more English words that begin with a *k* or have *k* as the third letter. Your mind is slowly churning: *kid, kiss, key*...

Did you think of any words with *k* as the third letter?

Probably not—it's difficult to recall these words. By contrast, words starting with a *k* spring effortlessly to mind. Naturally, words that start with a *k* must therefore be more prevalent in the English alphabet, right? Wrong. There are three times as many words that have *k* in the third position in the English language than there are words beginning with *k*.[5]

We see availability bias in a number of contexts when there is an availability *shock* in the news media. Two examples include the Fukushima Nuclear Disaster in Japan (see Figure 3.6) and the BP oil spill in the Gulf of Mexico (see Figure 3.7).

Pew Research Center conducts periodic sentiment polls on the use of nuclear power and oil and gas drilling in the United States. The polls clearly show how recent events—especially those spectacularly displayed in the media—can change implicit assessments of disaster probabilities.

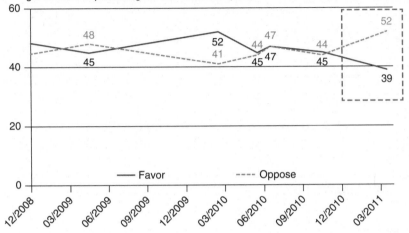

FIGURE 3.6 Promoting the Use of Nuclear Power in the US
Source: This graph is attributed to Jenkins Research, LLC. The data source is from Pew Research Center.

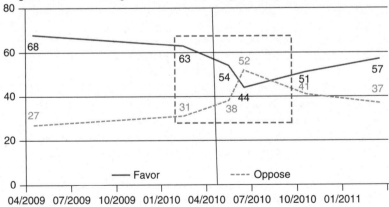

FIGURE 3.7 Allowing More Offshore Oil and Gas Drilling
Source: This graph is attributed to Jenkins Research, LLC. The data source is from Pew Research Center.

For example, sentiment on the use of nuclear power in the US shifts from an even split in June 2010 to 52 percent opposed and 39 percent in favor in March 2011, at the time of the Fukushima disaster. Similarly, in March 2010, 63 percent favored and 31 percent opposed offshore oil and gas drilling. However, after the BP oil spill disaster in the Gulf of Mexico, the June 2010 poll numbers showed 44 percent favored and 52 percent opposed offshore drilling.

Perhaps you don't believe this would affect investors? All one needs to do is read the Franklin Templeton Annual Global Investment Sentiment Survey, which asked investors—after the fact—to estimate the S&P 500 index performance for 2009 and 2010.[6] The survey said that 66 percent of investors believed the S&P 500 was down or flat in 2009, when the S&P was up 26.5 percent; 49 percent thought the market was down or flat in 2010, when the S&P was up 15.1 percent. The massive drawdown associated with the 2008 financial crisis obviously left a stinging—and available—impression on market participants.

Physical State

Are you a fellow coffee ~~addict~~ drinker? If we don't have our coffee in the morning, we feel sluggish, our heads start nodding, and crankiness abounds. And we are certainly not the exception. If you were to lay out a set of financials in front of us and demand an earnings forecast, we guarantee you that our answer would be highly dependent on our coffee consumption that morning. Physical state, while often overlooked by those discussing behavioral finance, is probably the most intuitive and compelling reason why a human expert can have the same set of facts, and yet arrive at different conclusions.

An interesting empirical study highlights the power of basic biological impulses (in this case, circadian rhythm) on the human mind. Bodenhausen conducts a study highlighting varying degrees of discrimination exhibited by individuals who self-identify as either "morning types" or "evening types."[7] Each individual is asked, at different times of the day, to state his opinion on the guiltiness of a suspect associated with an alleged crime. The descriptions of the suspects are purposely stereotyped in a way that should appeal to innate discrimination, thereby triggering System 1 heuristic decision-making.

The author tabulates the results for the perceived guilt by time of day for all participants in the study. Figure 3.8 breaks out the results for the 9:00 a.m. and 8:00 p.m. surveys for both morning and evening types. Morning types were more likely to give a suspect the benefit of the doubt when they were feeling bright and chipper early in the day, but much more

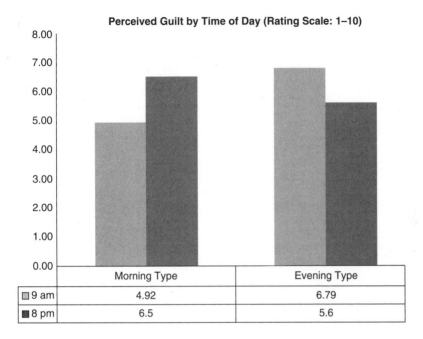

FIGURE 3.8   Perceived Guilt by Time of Day

likely to view the suspects as guilty when asked later in the day when their minds were wandering. Evening types exhibited the same pattern, but in reverse. Suspects were more likely to be considered guilty by the evening types in the morning, when they were presumably grumpier and less aware, but these same individuals were more lenient on suspects when asked in the evening, during a time when they were feeling more wakeful.

Overconfidence

Overconfidence, or the inability to appropriately calibrate our forecasts, is often cited as among the most robust empirical finding in psychology experiments.

Let's try a game.

Spend a couple of minutes identifying a low- and high-value answers to the questions in Table 3.1, such that you are 90 percent confident the answer lies in between your upper and lower bound. To be clear, answering "negative infinity" and "positive infinity," while clever, is missing the point of the game. You want to calibrate your upper and lower bound appropriately: not too cold, not too hot—just right. Go for it.

TABLE 3.1 Ten Question Overconfidence Test

	Low	High	Units
Martin Luther King's age at death	____	____	
Length of Nile River	____	____	Miles
Number of countries that are members of OPEC	____	____	
Number of books in the Old Testament	____	____	
Diameter of the moon	____	____	Miles
Weight of an empty Boeing 747	____	____	Pounds
Year in which Wolfgang Amadeus Mozart was born	____	____	
Gestation period (in days) of an Asian elephant	____	____	
Air distance from London to Tokyo	____	____	Miles
Deepest (known) point in the oceans	____	____	Feet

If you are like most people who play this game, you are reliably overconfident. Wes has collected ad-hoc experimental evidence on around 2,000 subjects who have taken this questionnaire. He finds that individuals typically get 30 percent correct, when a well-calibrated individual should, on average, get 90 percent correct, consistent with the 90 percent confidence interval. This low-scoring result holds even when Wes warns test-takers that prior test-takers have been systematically overconfident in their upper and lower bounds. Wes then encourages them to increase the bounds of their ranges. Of course, nobody listens, and on average, only three-tenths of the correct answers actually sit within the individual's confidence range. We are hard-wired to be overconfident.[8]

A common example of such overconfidence used to occur in the office when talking about sports. Jack is the resident sports expert. He is an avid fan of most sports and can easily recall random statistics for many teams and players. However, in the past, Jack used to be very certain about the outcome of games, and would let everyone know. But a funny thing happened to our "expert" when we began measuring his success rate: It was not as high as his confidence! Over the years (especially as we were writing this book), he learned to limit his "guarantees" with regard to the outcome of sporting events. While we all have some topic that we follow all the time (such as Jack with sports), the reality is that we may be overconfident in our own ability to predict future events. What cognitive biases are causing us to be overconfident? One answer may lie in our human desire to pursue and misuse useless information. Our brains immediately interpret more information as better information, which leads to more confidence, with no corresponding increase in forecast accuracy.

There is a compelling study by Bastardi and Shafir illustrating this effect that is appropriately titled, "On the pursuit and misuse of useless information."[9] The paper is filled with experiments that show our brain's inability to properly process information in a variety of circumstances. The abstract of the paper says it best:

"Decision makers often pursue noninstrumental information— information that appears relevant but, if simply available, would have no impact on choice. Once they pursue such information, people then use it to make their decision. Consequently, the pursuit of information that would have had no impact on choice leads people to make choices they would not otherwise have made."

Below is an example experiment from Bastardi and Shafir's research. The authors ask different groups to make a decision on a mortgage application. One group is faced with the following information set:

Group 1: Imagine that you are a loan officer at a bank reviewing the mortgage application of a recent college graduate with a stable, well-paying job and a solid credit history. The applicant seems qualified, but during the routine credit check you discover that for the last three months the applicant has not paid a $5,000 debt to his charge card account.

- Do you approve or reject the mortgage application?

Group 1 approves only 29 percent of the applications and rejects 71 percent.

The authors play a trick on the second group by leading them to believe they have more information. The hypothesis is that the subjects will interpret their supposed "special information" as information that can lead to a more accurate decision.

Group 2: Imagine that you are a loan officer at a bank reviewing the mortgage application of a recent college graduate with a stable, well-paying job and a solid credit history. The applicant seems qualified, but during the routine credit check you discover that for the last three months the applicant has not paid a debt to his charge card account. The existence of two conflicting reports makes it unclear whether the outstanding debt is for $5,000 or $25,000, and you cannot contact the credit agency until tomorrow to find out which is the correct amount.

- Do you approve or reject the mortgage application or wait?

Only 2 percent of the respondents approve the application, while 23 percent reject the application, and a majority (75 percent) chooses to wait for the additional information. For the majority who wait a day to get the additional information, the authors present them with the following tidbit:

The next day, they find out the amount is $5,000.

▪ **Do you approve or reject the mortgage application?**

For the majority who held out, 72 percent approve the application and 28 percent reject the application. In sum, for group 2, 56 percent approve the application and 44 percent reject the application. The approve rates are substantially higher than for group 1.

What is going on in this experiment? The authors have effectively given group 1 and group 2 the *exact same information set*, but because it is meted out over time, the second group perceives they have more information, which changes their decision-making process. Humans are cognitively inclined to overvalue information that requires effort or time to obtain.

To underscore the point that more information doesn't necessarily translate into better decisions, Professor Claire Tsai and colleagues directly test the relationship between information and forecast accuracy.[10] The *rational* hypothesis suggests that each information piece received will be appropriately weighted and integrated into a forecast (the *econ* hypothesis). Confidence in the forecast will be updated via appropriate statistical means (i.e., Bayesian updating). The *irrational* hypothesis is that humans will interpret more information as better information, without considering whether the additional information actually enhances their forecast ability (the *human* hypothesis). The prediction is that forecast accuracy will not improve as people receive more information, but their confidence in their forecast will increase linearly with more information.

The authors collect subjects who self-identify as being knowledgeable about college football. They present different subjects with up to 30 data points. The subjects are then asked to present a forecast for football game outcomes and their confidence in their forecast. To spice things up a bit, the researchers give the subjects the information set in such a way that they received the most predictive pieces of information first while each subsequent piece of information was less and less useful for predicting football game outcomes. In Figure 3.9, we highlight the summary results from the paper. The dark line represents the accuracy of subjects' forecasts over successive trials (where with each trial they are given more information); the dotted line represents the subjects' confidence with respect to their forecast.

The results of the study support the human hypothesis and reject the econ hypothesis. Humans incorrectly interpret more information as being better information than it really is. Their forecast accuracy does not improve

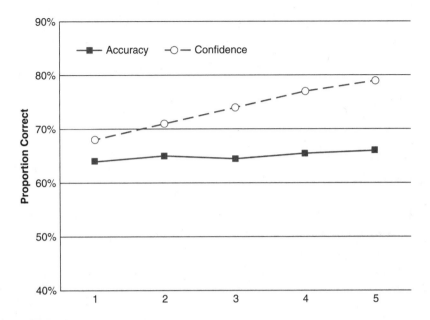

FIGURE 3.9 Overconfidence

with more information, but their confidence in their forecast grows linearly with the amount of information received.

How does the overconfidence effect play out in the financial realm? In another study, a team of scientists examines the effects of incremental information on market traders' forecasting ability and their confidence.[11] The researchers create an experimental trading lab where traders are randomly given different information sets with nine different levels of information. Information set I1 has no information about the market, while information set I9 is essentially inside information, with a nearly perfect picture about the future price of stocks. Once traders receive their information sets, they play a live trading game where the subjects try to maximize their returns. The intent of the experimental design is to capture an element of the real-world marketplace where some traders are better informed than others and these traders trade with each other in financial markets.

The results are shown in Figure 3.10, where the returns are shown net of the market. So a positive return means the investor beat the market, a negative number means the investor lost to the market, and a score of 0 means the investor tied the market. Amazingly, only the most informed traders with complete insider information can reliably beat the market. While it is unsurprising that a total insider could beat the market, it is striking that the partially informed traders do not. While the partially informed traders

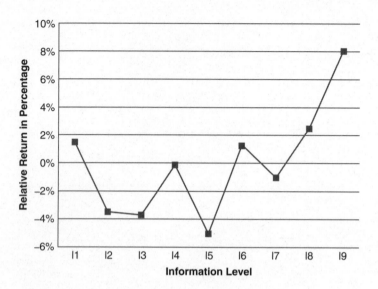

FIGURE 3.10 Nine Levels of Information

should outperform the market because they have privileged information, they do not, largely because they suffer from overconfidence and overvalue their own information set, and are therefore unable use it effectively. In fact, partially informed traders, on average, underperform. Uninformed investors, who know they have no information, are less likely to suffer from the cognitive bias of overconfidence, and thus end up achieving the market return, which in this experimental setting, is an admirable achievement.

What are we to make of this study? Is the takeaway that insider information is helpful for generating market-beating returns? Well, *no kidding*. In a game setting, we would all trade on insider information if we had it (and of course, assuming it was legal). However, in the real world, we must weigh the benefits of beating the market against the direct costs of being holed up in a cell wearing an orange jumpsuit and the indirect costs of having to shamefully stare into the jailhouse mirror every morning.

And for the rest of the traders in the marketplace with a partial information sets? These investors should be wary of interpreting their information as a way to enhance performance. If experimental evidence is any guide, it is more likely that additional information is causing us to make worse decisions, not better decisions. We must always ask ourselves if the information we are collecting is adding value by enhancing our forecasts or detracting from value by making us more overconfident.

In addition to correctly assessing the value of information we receive, we must avoid self-attribution bias, which is our innate desire to attribute good outcomes to skill and bad outcomes to bad luck. A good trade does not necessarily imply that the investor was better at "doing his homework," nor does a bad trade necessarily imply that the investor did a poor job of "doing his homework." And yet, our minds will often attribute a successful trade to our wonderful ability to collect and interpret mounds of filings submitted to the SEC, our ability to do the "hard work" of conducting channel checks on suppliers and customers, and our magnificent skill in being better than the average investor in the marketplace. Of course, when we endure a poor trade, we don't attribute the bad performance to a lack of skill, but instead, the bad trade can be squarely blamed on bad luck: an unforeseen change in government policy, or perhaps a remarkable change in the price of underlying commodities that "nobody could have seen coming."

A better approach for dealing with success and failures is to systematically discount success and overemphasize failures. Flip self-attribution bias on its head, or as Charlie Munger, vice chairman of Berkshire Hathaway, has promoted from time to time as a useful guiding principle, "Invert; always invert." While unappealing to most, reiterating that we are not as smart as we thought we were and realizing the pain of bad decisions can actually make us stronger, since it is a more accurate representation of reality. As the saying goes in the Marine Corps, "Pain is weakness leaving the body."

Overvaluing additional information and attributing success to our "personal skill" is a dangerous trait we should all monitor and be aware of. These two forces contribute to systematic and predictable overconfidence. For sports predictions, the bias is relatively harmless and amusing; however, the same bias, when deployed in the financial realm, can have disastrous consequences. Be wary of experts and their incremental information. It's not as valuable as you (and they) might think.

SUMMARY

In this chapter, we reviewed Wes's experience in Iraq, and how stressful combat conditions could drive soldiers to make irrational choices that were clearly inconsistent with their instinct to survive. In parallel, we examined specific biases that can impair human judgment. These include anchoring, framing, availability, effects of physical state, and overconfidence. The results, and takeaways, are strikingly similar. Human beings, including experts, suffer from subconscious biases. Unrelated data points and occurrences (ran out of coffee filters, CNBC reported earnings for Malaysian toothpaste companies, etc.) can subconsciously alter our decision-making. From bricklayer to hedge fund manager, the impacts are the same—we all suffer from subconscious bias.

NOTES

1. I. Simonson and A. Drolet, "Anchoring Effects on Consumers' Willingness-to-Pay and Willingness-to-Accept," *Journal of Consumer Research* 31 (2004): 681–690.
2. Daniel Kahneman, *Thinking, Fast and Slow* (New York: Macmillan, 2012), p. 119.
3. D. Ariely, *Predictably Irrational* (New York: Harper, 2010).
4. Ibid.
5. Amos Tversky and Daniel Kahneman, "Availability: A Heuristic for Judging Frequency and Probability," *Cognitive Psychology* 5 (1973): 207–233.
6. "The Franklin Templeton 2010/2011 Global Investor Sentiment Survey," Franklin Templeton Investments, accessed February 10, 2014, https://www.franklintempleton.com/investorsentiment.
7. G. Bodenhausen, "Stereotypes as Judgmental Heuristics: Evidence of Circadian Variations in Discrimination," *Psychological Science* 1 (1990): 319–322.
8. The answers are below:
     1. 39 yrs
     2. 4,187 miles
     3. 13 countries
     4. 39 books
     5. 2160 miles
     6. 390,000 pounds
     7. 1756
     8. 645 days
     9. 5,959 miles
    10. 36,198 feet
     From: J. E. Russo and P. J. H. Schowmaker, "Self-Test of Overconfidence," in *Confident Decision-Making* (London: Piatkus, 1989), p. 71, http://www.tim-richardson.net/misc/estimation_quiz.html.
9. C. A. Bastardi and E. Shafir, "On the Pursuit and Misuse of Useless Information," *Journal of Perspectives on Social Psychology* 75 (1998): 19–32.
10. Claire Tsai, Josh Klayman, and Reid Hastie, "Effects of Amount of Information on Judgment Accuracy and Confidence," *Organizational Behavioral and Human Decision Processes* 107 (2008): 97–105.
11. T. Bence, E. Scalas, J. Huber, and M. Kirchler, "The Value of Information in a Multiagent Market Model," *European Physical Journal B* 55 (2007): 115–120.

CHAPTER 4

Experts Tell Us Stories, Not Facts

"Just the facts, ma'am"

—Joe Friday, *Dragnet*

During World War II, the Allied forces set up airbases on the Melanesian Islands, which lay in a strategic zone off the northeastern coast of Australia. The Allies used the region as a staging area for troops and equipment during the war.[1]

At the time, these remote islands were populated by small groups of poor, indigenous peoples with limited exposure to other cultures. These isolated native populations were therefore highly curious when waves of foreign visitors from economically developed and technologically sophisticated cultures began to arrive. These nomadic armies also had an interest in the local natives, who were intimately familiar with the islands, and who could provide them with labor and other assistance as they worked to establish their military bases. In order to establish goodwill and engender the cooperation of the islanders, the foreigners began to share their commodities and supplies with them.

In this way, the natives were introduced to a huge variety of modern goods and items including jeeps, flashlights, pots and pans, knives, tents, washing machines, steel tools, tobacco, canned goods, medicine, clothing, and many other trappings of modern life. These were revolutionary technologies in the eyes of the natives, satisfying many basic needs and simplifying many daily tasks, and they dramatically enhanced the quality of life on the islands.

As time passed, the natives became increasingly enthusiastic about all the new cargo arriving on the islands, since they enjoyed the lifestyle changes and overall prosperity these modern goods generated. With these tremendous riches flowing to the local peoples, island life was good, and kept getting better. Over time, the islanders became increasingly reliant on the ongoing flow of supplies.

As the war wound down, however, the steady stream of goods onto the islands slowed to a trickle, and eventually came to an end. The airplanes stopped coming, the military bases and airstrips closed, and all the foreigners withdrew. The once spectacular flow of goods and material wealth had ceased completely. The islanders were left as they had been before.

The islanders were perplexed by the sudden change in their fortunes. What had happened to the great flow of wealth and material well-being they had enjoyed for so many years? What accounted for this unwelcome change that had occurred, and was there anything they could do to restore the material prosperity that had prevailed previously? The islanders were trying to make sense of their new world, and started identifying ways in which they might remedy their situation based on what they knew.

The Melanesian natives knew that things happen for a reason. They were not stupid. What was the nature of the connection between the foreigners, their actions, and the cargo? From the islanders' perspective, there appeared to be several possible explanations for what they had observed over time. For example, it seemed likely the foreigners were acquainted with certain methods of generating the great flow of wealth. The islanders had observed the foreigners do many different things, some of which perhaps were related to the arrival of the cargo in some way. What was the key?

The foreigners had come to the islands and built roads, bases, and airfields with towers overseeing illuminated landing strips, where airplanes filled with goods came to land, and were seen to accumulate. They conducted various marching drills, while holding weapons on their shoulders and wearing distinctive clothing. They hoisted ceremonial banners. The foreigners were very different, and did a lot of strange things.

The islanders reasoned that perhaps there was some sort of magic or deity involved in the process of wealth creation. Perhaps there was even some kind of connection to spirits or the natives' ancestors? Regardless, there appeared to be a clear connection between the foreigners and their various activities and the cargo. The natives reasoned that they were capable of doing everything they had seen the foreigners do. If some of the various rituals the islanders had observed could be recreated, these might very well activate the magical flow of materials to the island. And so they developed a strategy to get the magic, ancestors, or deities involved: They set about emulating the foreigners, and recreating their customs and rituals. They did this in various ways.

The islanders recreated the airstrips, marking them with sticks, and illuminating them with torches. They built thatched huts along the runways, outfitting these with bamboo, vines, and tin cans strung on wires to mimic control towers with radio antennae, including a place for a man to sit and wear coconut earphones to communicate with the airplanes. They stood on the landing strips making landing signals to attract the planes. They built airplanes out of sticks, leaves, and grass, in order to attract other airplanes. They made airplane sounds. They replicated complex marching drills and conducted these prescribed dances while holding makeshift firearms.

Everything was perfect. The configuration of the runways was accurate, the airplanes were highly realistic, and the huts were faithful reproductions of control towers. The drills and the marching ceremonies had been flawlessly reproduced. All was as it had been during the prosperous days. Yet, despite their elaborate preparations, the natives still lacked something crucial and fundamental, because, of course, the planes failed to land and the cargo failed to materialize.

It was true that there was a connection between the rituals of the foreigners and the arrival of the cargo. The natives were right about that. The rituals did accompany the arrival of the cargo. And in some sense the rituals were also required as a condition for the arrival of the cargo. But they did not independently cause the arrival of the cargo. This was the flaw in the story. The real reasons the cargo came were much more subtle and complex, and related to hidden factors that were completely removed from the experience of the islanders and their explanations. The true nature of the rituals was misinterpreted by the natives as being causative, when the reality was totally different.[2]

And while we might consider the natives naïve, we also need to recognize these natives are only human, and behave just as other humans behave. They created a plausible explanation, essentially out of thin air, and believed it.

Humans believe in stories at the expense of evidence all the time—even in our modern society. And these stories abound. Below we list a sampling of "stories" that aren't grounded in facts:[3]

- Don't swim after eating.
- Shaving thickens hair.
- The Great Wall of China is visible from space.
- Toilets flush backward on the other side of the equator.

People, in general, are wired to try to understand their world. When we lack a cogent interpretation of events, this generates cognitive strain, and we struggle to make sense of things. Humans thus crave a coherent narrative; the human mind likes to resolve conflicts that are not understood or cause cognitive dissonance and create disharmony. In other words, humans like *stories* to explain things!

For instance, loathing ambiguity, the mind is predisposed, after the fact, to invent stories that fit unexpected outcomes. Once we have created a story that seems to fit our specific circumstances particularly well, then we tend to believe that story, and it becomes our reality. The problem is that our stories sometimes simply do not reflect reality.

Clearly, we can sometimes be swayed by a good story, despite a lack of evidence or even contravening evidence. In the investing context, we see a similar phenomenon: story-based investing is everywhere, but evidence-based investing is scarce. But, why? One would expect that financial decisions, which can have a large influence on our well-being, would be grounded in evidence and not vulnerable to our innate belief in storytelling. This would seem not to be the case. Throughout the balance of this chapter, we will explore story bias and how this bias can be reflected in the financial marketplace.

STORY-BASED INVESTING

The three of us all have young daughters who always ask, "Daddy, how did we get these presents under the Christmas tree?" We respond with, "Oh, Santa dropped them off." Our daughters then say, "How did Santa bring them here?" We reply, "On his sleigh, guided by his reindeers. Of course." Our daughters consider this, and then respond, "Oh, yeah, that makes sense. He even ate the cookies we left by the fireplace and his reindeers ate the carrots we left outside." The circle is complete, and the story is airtight.

Human beings have strong preferences for coherent stories and often build powerful narratives to help interpret complex situations. In our daughters' cases, the impossible physics of the Santa story will cause the story to break down over time, but the powerful Santa Claus narrative will likely extend well beyond what many would consider its "rational life." The Santa Claus story is one that appeals to many young children,[4] but it is not just children who suffer from a strong belief in stories; adults are highly susceptible as well.

The basis for our persistent belief in stories, in spite of evidence suggesting a story is unbelievable, has perplexed researchers for many years. Consider the range of fantastic human superstitions, which are pervasive in society. The behavioral psychologist B. F. Skinner and several colleagues demonstrated that our innate need for superstition is deeply ingrained in our primal brains.[5] To make the point, Skinner studied one of the more powerful brains in the animal kingdom—the pigeon.

Skinner put hungry pigeons in a cage and dispensed food pellets to them every five seconds. Now, as we all know from our urban sidewalk experiences, pigeons will naturally wander around any space looking for food, and will do so in predictably pigeon-like ways. One pigeon might step to the left and then step to the right; another pigeon might jump, land, and then jump again. In the experiment, following these random movements a food pellet will appear, consistent with a five-second release pattern. After a few rounds of engaging in the same random activities and earning a series of food pellets, each pigeon develops an internal story: Some particular deliberate action it took in the cage is causing food pellets to pop out of the feeder. Pigeons that randomly kick to the right start to believe that kicking to the right releases the pellet. Pigeons that kick to the left continue the same pattern with the opposite foot, and so on.

Amazingly, once a pigeon establishes a superstition, it is exceedingly difficult to train the pigeon out of the story. Skinner attempts to give the pigeons evidence that their superstition is worthless (e.g., only releasing pellets when the right foot is NOT kicked), but the pigeons continue with their story-based ways. Evidence has a hard time entering the decision-making process once a behavior has been established.

EVIDENCE-BASED INVESTING

Think you are different from a pigeon? Pigeons aren't the only animals suffering from story bias. Wes's uncle is convinced that a Dallas Cowboys victory during the Thanksgiving Day football game is a great signal for the stock market. The logic is as follows: The Cowboys are "America's Team" and if America's Team is doing well, people are happier and they spend more money. Wes's uncle really believes in this story, despite the consistent reminder he receives from all of our wives, who are life-long Eagles fans, and who highlight the evidence: Since the turn of the century, the Cowboys prediction measure is batting 9/14, or 64 percent. This means that over the past 14 years, when the Cowboys win the Thanksgiving game, 9 times out of 14 the market was positive the following year (see Table 4.1). This sounds pretty good until you consider that over the past 87 years (1927 to 2013) there is a 72.4 percent chance the market is positive. Clearly, the Cowboys indicator is bunk.

So Wes's uncle might have told himself a great story, but it certainly isn't backed by robust empirical evidence. And even if it were backed by evidence, you would be hard-pressed to raise investment capital to invest in the strategy. Or maybe you wouldn't. We would hope, however, that the "Dallas Cowboys" indicator is a bit far-fetched for most. How about the "52-week low" stock screen? Many of our stock-picking friends love

TABLE 4.1   Performance of Dallas Cowboy Victory Signal (2000 to 2013)

Year	S&P 500 Return	Cowboy Outcome	Year Ahead Return	Correct Prediction?
2000	−8.34%	Loss	−11.88%	Yes
2001	−11.88%	Loss	−21.78%	Yes
2002	−21.78%	Win	28.72%	Yes
2003	28.72%	Loss	10.98%	No
2004	10.98%	Win	5.23%	Yes
2005	5.23%	Loss	15.69%	No
2006	15.69%	Win	5.76%	Yes
2007	5.76%	Win	−36.46%	No
2008	−36.46%	Win	26.49%	Yes
2009	26.49%	Win	15.35%	Yes
2010	15.35%	Loss	2.11%	No
2011	2.11%	Win	16.00%	Yes
2012	16.00%	Loss	32.39%	No
2013	32.39%	Win	13.69%	Yes

this screen, thinking that 52-week-low stocks are "cheap," on average, and therefore must offer the potential for great return relative to other stocks in the investment universe. Unfortunately, "52-week-low stocks" are virtually synonymous with what academic researchers call "low-momentum stocks." Low-momentum stocks, for those who shy away from reading academic finance journals, have been shown to be one of the worst-performing groups of stocks one can choose from.

There are many other stock market superstitions—sell in May and go away; let your winners run, but cut your losses; head and shoulders patterns; this is a stock-pickers' market; the Santa Claus rally; invest in what you know; do your homework; buy with a margin of safety; and so forth. Some of these stories are backed by evidence; others are not. We should not believe these stories indiscriminately, just because they seem to make sense or some ostensible authority figure insists they are true. The main point is that one's investment process should not be based on a story, but rather, on an evidence-based process that demonstrates robustness over time. Below, we outline three common and compelling market stories where empirical evidence is lacking (there are many more).

Myth #1 Warren Buffett Beats Ben Graham

Ben Graham, Warren Buffett's mentor and original employer, had a strict focus on margin of safety. Graham's investment philosophy was to *always buy cheap* and never stray from a low price strategy. The essence of Ben Graham is captured in two of his recommended investment approaches:

1. Purchase stocks at less than their net current asset value, a strategy Graham considered "almost unfailingly dependable and satisfactory."[6]
2. Create a portfolio of stocks a minimum of 30 stocks meeting specific price-to-earnings criteria (below 10) and specific debt-to-equity criteria (below 50 percent).[7]

Both of these investment approaches maintain an overarching theme involving paying a low price, independent of quality.

When Buffett came in to the spotlight, he suggested a wrinkle in Graham's original approach. Buffet's own words capture the flavor of his investment approach:

"It's far better to buy a wonderful company at a fair price than a fair company at a wonderful price."[8]

In a Buffett world, Coke at a price-to-earnings ratio of 20 might be a value stock, but the textile firm Berkshire Hathaway may be overpriced at a P/E of 5. In a Graham world, Berkshire Hathaway is always the better bet. Anecdotally, it is easy to claim that Buffett was the clear winner in the horse race against Graham. But are we suffering from availability bias or story bias when we make this conjecture?[9]

What does the actual evidence have to say on the subject?

We can empirically verify whether a Buffett or Graham philosophy has been more effective over the past 37 years. To do so, we need to quantify Warren Buffett and Ben Graham's strategies in a systematic way. Joel Greenblatt, famous for his book, *The Little Book that Beats the Market*, tells a story about a systematic investment approach that encapsulates the Warren Buffet mantra of trying to "buy a wonderful business at a fair price." Greenblatt's formula is straightforward: Rank all stocks on their earnings before interest and taxes relative to their total enterprise value (EBIT/TEV). EBIT/TEV serves as the "cheapness" indicator for a given security (labeled "Graham" in Table 4.2). Next, measure the "quality" of a firm by calculating the ratio of EBIT to capital (labeled "Quality" in Table 4.2), which satisfies Buffett's own criteria that the "more appropriate measure of managerial economic performance is return on equity capital."[10] To generate the Warren Buffett clone strategy, we simply average the EBIT/TEV and EBIT/CAPITAL ranks and then purchase the top-ranked stocks based on the combined "cheapness" and "quality" ranking (labeled "Buffett" in Table 4.2).

TABLE 4.2   Performances of the Three Strategies

	Buffett	Graham	Quality	S&P 500 TR
CAGR	13.94%	15.95%	10.37%	10.46%
Standard Deviation	16.93%	17.28%	17.04%	15.84%
Downside Deviation	12.02%	11.88%	11.35%	11.16%
Sharpe Ratio	0.55	0.64	0.35	0.37
Sortino Ratio (MAR = 5%)	0.80	0.96	0.56	0.56
Worst Drawdown	−36.85%	−37.25%	−47.15%	−50.21%

The performance metrics in Table 4.2 are calculated over the 1974 to 2011 timeframe and the universe consists only of investable firms (we eliminate small/micro caps). The far left column is the performance of Warren Buffett stocks as captured by Greenblatt's combined cheapness and quality measure. The second column represents the Graham cheap-stock strategy using only EBIT/TEV as the sorting variable. The third column is the stand-alone quality measure. The fourth column is the S&P 500 total return index. Each active strategy ranks stocks on the respective metric every June 30th and rebalances annually. The results reported represent the performance of the top decile of stocks for a given measure.

The performance for the Buffett formula (average of cheapness and quality) is admirable over the time period analyzed. Annual growth rates are almost 3.5 percent higher per year than the S&P 500 benchmark, and the Sharpe and Sortino risk-reward calculations are also stronger. But the Graham strategy (cheapness) outperforms on nearly every metric. The Graham strategy beats the market by over 5 percent a year, on average, and risk-reward metrics are much stronger than both the benchmark and the Buffett strategy. The evidence supports the argument that the original Graham value-investment philosophy is superior to the updated Buffet value-investment philosophy.

How is it possible that Graham beats Buffett? The answer lies in the quality component of the Buffett philosophy. If we examine the quality strategy's stand-alone performance we notice that the results are slightly weaker than the benchmark, suggesting that any strategy that, based on a quality metric, moves out of cheap stocks, and into expensive stocks, will correspondingly dilute overall performance. We see this borne out in the Buffett results, which represent a mix of a quality component and a low-price component. As we summarize in *Quantitative Value*, "[an equally weighted combination of quality and price algorithm] systematically overpays for quality. It is structurally flawed, leading us to fish in the wrong pond." The lesson from the evidence is that Graham was correct, on average. And yet, the story of "value investing" has slowly evolved away from strictly buying cheap stocks to buying stocks across the price spectrum based on quality attributes that are not useful if a stock is not cheap. This is effectively the idea behind "growth at a reasonable price" investing. Unfortunately, this revamped value-investing story is not backed by robust empirical evidence. Warren Buffett is merely an anecdote associated with a great story, but the tale told by Graham (buy cheap stocks) is backed by evidence and therefore should maintain its status as the "golden rule of value investing."

Myth #2 Economic Growth Drives Stock Returns

Should investors favor strong economic growth? Of course they should if they want to earn high returns. Strong growth drives profits, which drives returns. This practically goes without saying in the investing world. If economic vitality didn't matter, all the time spent pontificating over economic figures and developing growth forecasts associated with these estimates would be a complete waste of time, right? And that's obviously wrong, because astute professional investors are too smart to waste time on activity that doesn't matter or add value.

Not so fast.

We're going to let you in on a secret: Investors focused on economic growth are wasting their time. Jay Ritter tells a compelling *evidence-based story* that economic growth *doesn't benefit* stockholders.[11] If anything, the evidence suggests a negative correlation between equity returns and GDP growth.[12] Figure 4.1 shows the relation between real equity returns and real per capita GDP growth for 16 countries over the 1900 to 2002 period—over a 100-year testing period!

The figure highlights the fact there is virtually no relationship between stock returns and GDP growth. And yet, investors are so focused on the powerful narrative that GDP growth increases corporate profits, they forget to review the underlying theory or evidence sustaining this bogus story. From a theory perspective, the only way a firm increases stockholder value is by investing firm capital in positive net present value projects. And it is unclear why strong economic growth will contribute to a firm's ability to identify more, or higher yielding, investment projects in a competitive economy (such as which projects the CEO decides to undertake). In some cases, economic growth could make this more difficult.

Buffett made this point painfully clear in his famous 1999 article in *Fortune* magazine. First, the Oracle of Omaha rattles off a handful of transformative high-growth industries that translated into terrible investments (e.g., airlines, automobiles, radios, and televisions). He then leaves us with a profound statement that lays out a logical case that investors shouldn't fall in love with growth for growth's sake: *"The key to investing is not assessing how much an industry is going to affect society, or how much it will grow,*

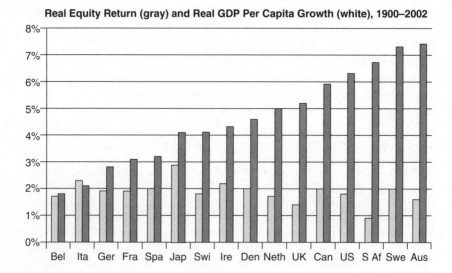

Real Equity Return (gray) and Real GDP Per Capita Growth (white), 1900–2002

FIGURE 4.1   Real Equity and Real GDP Per Capita Growth

but rather determining the competitive advantage of any given company and, above all, the durability of that advantage. The products or services that have wide, sustainable moats around them are the ones that deliver rewards to investors." [13]

Buffet reminds investors why they shouldn't cling to macroeconomic growth stories. So, on which area should investors focus? As Ritter says quite succinctly: "current earnings yields." Translated for non-finance geeks, this simply means price. And as any intelligent investor will tell you, the price you pay has everything to do with the returns one will receive. If investors pay a high price for a given asset, they can expect low returns; if the same investors pay a low price for a given asset, they can expect high returns. The real story here is that high equity returns are earned by investors who focus on paying low prices for firms with strong abilities to invest in positive net present value projects. It may be that the best prices can be had in times of low economic growth, whereas we tend to overpay in a growing economy. The idea that strong economic growth translates into strong stock returns is a superstition, and is not backed by evidence.

Myth #3 The Payout Superstition

Every quarter, boards across America wrestle with the complex question of dividend policy. Perhaps the company has excess cash that should be paid out as a dividend? Or perhaps cash should be directed to high net-present-value projects? It's a nuanced and sophisticated debate, which makes it the perfect breeding ground for generating investor superstitions.

Quant heavyweights Cliff Asness (AQR) and Rob Arnott (Research Affiliates) have noted that market observers often predict that low-dividend payout ratios imply higher earnings growth in the future.[14] Conversely, when dividend payout ratios are high, commentators suggest that earnings growth will slow in subsequent years. We call this story the *payout superstition.*

Again, the logic seems to make sense: If companies retain earnings (i.e., low dividend payout) and plow them back into promising projects, earnings growth should be higher in the future; conversely, if companies don't see any growth opportunities, they will push cash back to shareholders (i.e., high dividend payout) and future earnings shouldn't experience robust growth.

The payout superstition is a great story, but is this really how the world works from an empirical standpoint?

Arnott and Asness looked at historical payout ratios and earnings growth of stocks broadly representative of the market. Figure 4.2 is a scatterplot showing payout ratios and subsequent 10-year real earnings growth from 1946 to 2001.

The evidence definitely indicates that there is a relationship between the payout ratio and future earnings growth. But it is not the relationship we expected. Instead, it is higher dividend-payout ratios that predict higher

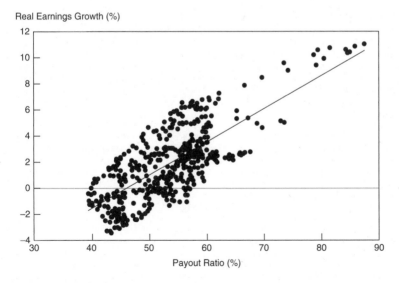

FIGURE 4.2 Scatterplot of Payout Ratio vs. Subsequent 10-Year Real Earnings Growth, 1946–2001 Data

growth, while lower payout ratios predict lower growth—the opposite of the payout superstition. As a two-year-old says after dropping food from the table: "*Uh-oh.*" The results are completely backward—it's precisely the opposite of what we expect.

Asness and Arnott suggest a few hypotheses for why this might be true:

- Since managers don't like to cut dividends, if they are concerned about the sustainability of earnings in the future they would not offer a higher dividend today; a higher payout ratio is a signal that they think future prospects look poor.
- When earnings are not paid out, cash is used to finance poor investments (malinvestment), leading to reduced earnings growth.
- When managers hold cash, it may signal "empire building," where managers try to increase their power, rather than act to benefit shareholders.

Arnott and Assness's analysis suggests that if a firm has extra cash, there are reasonable arguments why they should pay out cash as dividends, rather than hold it or invest it in disastrous projects that could destroy value. In a world where malinvestment and empire building are pervasive, dividends might provide a valuable signal about a firm's shareholder policies. And perhaps mischievous corporate managers are exploiting the payout superstition for their own benefit?

The Moral of the Stories

The number of fairytales, rules of thumb, and magic charms sold in the financial markets are too numerous to list. We've highlighted three of the more coherent and believable stories in the marketplace that are called into question by empirical facts. The lesson is clear for all of us who enjoy a great investment pitch: In order to be good investors, we need to appreciate our natural preference for coherent stories over evidence that conflicts with those stories. Don't be the pigeon doing a "pellet voodoo dance," when it has already been shown that the pellet voodoo dance doesn't work.

THE RECAP: WHY EXPERTS FAIL

Once again, the expert's hypothesis is based on the following flawed assumptions:

- Qualitative information increases forecast accuracy.
- More information increases forecast accuracy.
- Experience and intuition enhance forecast accuracy.

As we have shown thus far in this book, the assumptions underlying the expert's hypothesis are empirically invalid: "Soft," or qualitative, information doesn't enhance forecasting ability; more information doesn't enhance forecasting ability; and experience doesn't enhance forecasting ability.

Systematic models work because the human mind is reliably unreliable.

Let us push crushing reality aside for a moment, and make the claim that most of us can be truly evidence-based decision makers who are not influenced by stories that capture our imagination and impact our decision-making ability. If we are truly empirical-based individuals, the evidence overwhelmingly suggests that we should all be using models and other algorithms to implement and execute decisions, rather than relying on experts.

But who is ready to concede that a machine is better at making decisions? You are probably like us: The idea of scrapping our years of hard-won experience is awfully hard to swallow.

Humans naturally seek to fulfill what Maslow—famous for developing the human hierarchy of needs[15]—calls our innate need for esteem and self-actualization. We want to feel that our opinions and judgment matter. Recognizing the fact that simple models outperform experts directly challenges our self-directed desire to achieve goals, gain confidence, and feel a sense of achievement. We want to feel like our efforts are worthwhile, but we often devote little effort to understanding if our frenetic activity actually adds value.

Consider the act of banging one's head against the wall for 10 hours a day, seven days a week. Banging your head against the wall involves a lot of activity, but because the outcome of this activity is clearly "bad," it is easy to know that this focused effort is a waste of time. However, what if we are spending 10 hours a day reading SEC filings of companies? Is this intense activity valuable? Are we learning anything that is actually helping us to make better stock picks? A lot of investors assume it is, but have they ever systematically reviewed this assumption? Maybe this, or other, so-called "value-add" activities performed by experts is equivalent to banging one's head against the wall? Perhaps these activities are not contributing to value at all, but are actually detracting from value?

We can't say with certainty, but based on the bevy of tests previously cited, we can conjecture that while the analyst reading SEC documents all day is clearly collecting more information, the information may do nothing to enhance the analyst's forecasting ability. In fact, it is quite likely that the additional information detracts from his ability, as the analyst becomes systematically overconfident in his forecast of the future. Overall, any potential information edge that may exist can easily be overwhelmed by costs associated with cognitive bias issues.

WHY NOT USE MODELS?

Imagine you are watching Gary Kasparov, Russia's preeminent chess master, taking on IBM's Deep Blue, a cold, calculating box designed by a bunch of geeks. During the match, Gary is sweating it out, smiling when he makes a nice move, and cringing in pain when Deep Blue takes his queen. We see that Gary is like us. He is *familiar*; the machine is just an inhuman metal box. The machine has no emotion, no feelings, no empathy. Who do we want to win the match? We want Gary. He's like us, and we have a preference for the familiar (yes, another bias, we know). Nobody wants a computer to win.

And so what if the machine is actually better at chess than a human? We get it: Deep Blue with its ability to analyze 200 million positions per second, can best a human opponent. Does that mean we want a chess-playing computer mainframe making our life-and-death medical decisions—*even if the evidence suggests it should?* Probably not. Humans might be willing to put up with a flawed, but familiar human, because we empathize with flesh and blood. If the heart surgeon kills my aunt because he accidently tied the tubes the wrong way, that's unfortunate, and I'm angry, but "people make mistakes, we're all human." But imagine if a robot performs surgery on my aunt and she dies because the robot tied the tubes the wrong way. My immediate reaction: "Who in the heck thought it was a good idea to have a robot perform heart surgery—Where's my lawyer!?!" However, the truth is, increasingly in medicine the robot is much less likely to make such a mistake, on average. We should be rooting for machines that make fewer errors, not excusing human error.

Even if one buys the argument that models can be useful, one might object that models are too limited and cannot be applied in sophisticated contexts like investment decision-making. What, for example, is the algorithm going to say when we face a unique situation the world has never seen? This time is *actually* different. The story is that the human expert can adapt and create on-the-fly modifications to the model that creates value. This well-trodden, but empirically busted, rebuttal against algorithms is deemed the *broken-leg theory* and relies on the false premise that humans don't suffer from System 1 flaws.

Under the broken leg theory, if we are competing against a model to judge whether someone will, say, go to the movies, and we happen to know this person has a broken leg and the model does not account for this, then we can use this unique, incremental knowledge to make a better judgment than the machine. One problem with this view is that it is difficult to know whether a given information signal (which may be more nuanced than a broken leg) is dispositive and reliable. Thus, we continue to extend and apply our judgment over and over again in different cases, and override the model when we shouldn't.

Sure, knowledge of the broken leg helps us beat the model. Discretionary decision makers are often able to identify the value-enhancing modifications that can theoretically outperform a simple model in specific cases. However, they simultaneously identify value-destroying modifications that cause them to underperform in other cases. Discretionary experts' inclination to "modify" simple models resembles a bag of Lay's Potato Chips—the experts "can't eat just one" modification. They might add a positive "broken leg" modification, but they also add negative modifications. And as the evidence suggests, allowing a human to engage in ad-hoc "gut" decision-making is not a good idea.

Of course, the great irony is that an expert can read and understand the evidence on systematic versus ad-hoc decision-making and agree that decisions should be made systematically with a simple model. However, overconfidence, arguably the bias that hurts experts the most, causes these "special" experts to believe they are the exception to the rule. While others can't beat the simple model, they can.

The problem is that we *all* believe we are better than average. The crushing reality is, "You are less beautiful than you think."[16]

- *Are you a better driver than average? 93 percent of US citizens think so, too.*[17]
- *Are you a great teacher? 94 percent of professors think so, too.*[18]
- *Are you a better than average stock picker? Of course you are.*

Relegating your decision-making processes to systems requires a massive dose of humble pie. Most—if not all—experts are unable to consume this dish. But to be a better decision maker, we must eat our humble pie. As we have shown in the previous chapters, in order for decision-making to be effective, it must be systematic. And the only systematic thing about humans is our flaws. Therefore, it is best to leave the stock picking to a simple model, which over time, will most likely outperform experts.

SUMMARY

Chapter 4 is about how stories sometimes do not reflect reality. We began with a description of a story created by Melanesian Islanders that failed to bring cargo back to their islands. Next, we discussed how children believe Santa's story (although grownups don't), and how B. F. Skinner's pigeons also created stories around meaningless rituals that preceded the delivery of food pellets. We also discussed meaningless rituals that humans imbue with predictive value, such as the Dallas Cowboys indicator. Even Warren Buffett seems to be selling a story about paying more for high-quality companies that doesn't seem to hold up based on the evidence. We also reviewed other finance stories that seem to make sense, but just aren't true, including the stories that economic growth and lower payout ratios drive higher future stock returns. Because stories are so compelling, we must be on constant guard to prevent ourselves from believing in something that isn't based on evidence.

NOTES

1. Paul Raffaele, "In John We Trust," *Smithsonian Magazine* (February 2006), http://www.smithsonianmag.com/people-places/in-john-they-trust-109294882/.
2. Peter Worsley, "50 Years Ago: Cargo Cults of Melanesia," *Scientific American* (April 20, 2009), http://www.scientificamerican.com/article/1959-cargo-cults-melanesia/.
3. http://www.snopes.com/oldwives/hourwait.asp; http://www.snopes.com/oldwives/hairgrow.asp; http://www.snopes.com/science/greatwall.asp; http://www.snopes.com/science/coriolis.asp, accessed April 20, 2014.
4. In Wes's case, he believed in Santa Claus until the age of 14—and he still does believe at times. Physics be damned!
5. B. F. Skinner, "Superstition in the Pigeon," *Journal of Experimental Psychology* 38 (1948): 168–172.
6. B. Graham and D. Dodd, *Security Analysis* (New York: McGraw-Hill, 1934).
7. B. Graham, "A Conversation with Benjamin Graham," *Financial Analysts Journal* 32 (1976): 20–23.
8. W. Buffett, "Chairman's Letter," Berkshire Hathaway Inc. Annual Report, 1989.
9. "Buffett's Alpha," a 2013 working paper by Frazzini, Kabiller, and Pedersen, identified that Buffett buys cheap, high-quality firms. So, empirically, one could argue that Buffett is in fact a Ben Graham cheap-stock investor.
10. W. Buffett, "Chairman's Letter," Berkshire Hathaway Inc. Annual Report, 1977.
11. J. R. Ritter, "Economic Growth and Equity Returns," *Pacific-Basin Finance Journal* 13 (2005): 489–503.
12. Ritter find a cross-sectional correlation of −0.37 for the compounded real return on equities and the compounded growth rate of real per capital GDP for 16 countries over the 1900–2002 period.
13. Mr. Buffett on the Stock Market, Warren Buffett, and Carol Loomis. http://archive.fortune.com/magazines/fortune/fortune_archive/1999/11/22/269071/index.htm, accessed 4/20/2014.
14. R. Arnott and C. Asness, "Surprise: Higher Payout Rates = Higher Growth Rates," *Financial Analysts Journal* 59 (2003): 70–87.
15. A. H. Maslow, "A Theory of Human Motivation," *Psychological Review* 50 (1943): 370–96.

16. Ozgun Atasoy, "You Are Less Beautiful Than You Think," *Scientific American* (May 21, 2013), http://www.scientificamerican.com/article/you-are-less-beautiful-than-you-think/.

17. O. Svenson, "Are We All Less Risky and More Skillful than Our Fellow Drivers?" *Acta Psychologica* 47 (1980): 143–148.

18. P. Cross, "Not Can, but Will College Teaching Be Improved?" *New Directions for Higher Education* 17 (2006): 1–15.

Two

How You Can Beat the Experts

art One is meant to give readers the confidence to question expert opinion and to believe in the power of systematic decision-making. Part Two outlines how individuals, armed with evidence-based models and the discipline to follow these models, can beat the experts. Part Two begins with an outline for why a do-it-yourself approach to investing makes sense. Chapters 6, 7, and 8 are dedicated to outlining ways in which a DIY Financial Advisor can build a fully integrated retirement portfolio after considering asset allocation, risk-management, and security selection elements. Chapter 9 provides an overview of how to formulate a reasonable do-it-yourself solution. Finally, in Chapter 10 we end Part Two with a discussion of why we are actually unlikely to implement a do-it-yourself solution, even though it is probably the rational way to invest our hard-earned wealth.

CHAPTER 5

A Framework for Investment Decisions

"We are prone to overestimate how much we understand about the world and to underestimate the role of chance in events."
—Dan Kahneman, *Thinking, Fast and Slow*

We hope that Part One left you with a central message: We can beat the experts. Experts are biased and overconfident. Many years of experience are not something to be worshipped but something to be questioned. A long history of success does not guarantee future success; instead, it is a red flag for bias and overconfidence. We don't need an expert to make good decisions; we need a psychology coach. We know overconfidence is an overwhelming influence in decision-making, and this effect is often magnified for experts—unless it is rigorously contained. Many successful experts aren't even aware they are overconfident, which means they almost certainly have not put systematic processes in place to counteract overconfidence. We can do better and beat the experts. In order to beat the experts what we need is an evidence-based systematic decision-making process.

Yet the experts themselves can create additional barriers to adopting such processes. After all, the experts don't want you to follow an evidence-based systematic process—it would cut them out of the picture and eliminate their rationale for charging you a fee. We need to rigorously defend against their influential tactics. Financial service professionals utilize the following techniques to influence us into hiring them to make decisions on our behalf:

- *Fear tactics.* "If you don't use our services, there is a chance you may lose your entire nest egg. We keep you diversified and have all the accountants and lawyers to ensure you are viable in the future."
- *Greed tactics.* "You only get access to these trades by being a customer of the firm. These opportunities are saved for our best customers."
- *Complexity tactics.* "Do you really think you can beat the market by using a simple model? We have armies of MBAs and PhDs doing research all day long looking for opportunities. If you want to beat the market, you need to hire us so you can access their capabilities."
- *Relationship tactics.* "Jim, you've been with the firm for 20 years. You trust us, right? Let me take you out to lunch and we can discuss this ridiculous decision to do-it-yourself."

Before you get snared in a trap set by a financial "expert," reread Part One of this book. Next, identify if the expert is pitching you on her services by leveraging fear, greed, complexity, or relationship tactics. If you sense a trap, run the other way as fast as you can (and don't forget your wallet!). And if you simply don't have the time to deal with your portfolio, focus on experts that utilize systematic evidence-based approaches in their investment portfolio.

But let's say you are ready to be the chief investment officer of your family office, whether it has assets of $10,000 or $5,000,000,000. You want to learn; you are willing to work hard; and you have eaten a healthy dose of humble pie. The next question is the following: "How do I manage my portfolio?" The process to becoming a DIY family office is straightforward:

- Step 1: Assess your current advisor/broker relationships.
- Step 2: Stick to the FACTS:
  - Fees
  - Access
  - Complexity
  - Taxes
  - Search
- Step 3: Understand portfolio management fundamentals:
  - Asset allocation
  - Risk management
  - Security selection

The remainder of this chapter is dedicated to outlining each of these steps in greater detail.

ASSESSING AN ADVISOR IS DIFFICULT

When it comes to investing, there is a simple question we often ask: What would Charlie Munger do? Mr. Munger is Warren Buffett's better half at Berkshire Hathaway, a multibillionaire and a master of human psychology and decision-making. As we mentioned earlier, one of Charlie's favorite approaches to decision-making is to "invert, always invert." What Charlie means by this is that when evaluating a solution, instead of asking, "Why is X a good solution?" we should turn the question around, and work backward from the inverted question. For example, we might also consider, "Why is X *not a* good solution?" Inverting the question, and turning it over in different ways, helps us understand X in a new way and may give use reasons to reconsider our acceptance of X. This inversion of perspective illuminates the opposite of what others are looking at and provides a deeper understanding of potential solutions.

When Charlie talks, we listen. So instead of identifying all the reasons why investors can benefit from investment advisors (which everyone can cite chapter and verse), we decided to come up with a list of 10 things people don't like about their financial advisors. Here is the list of 10 things that destroy the potential value of the financial experts we hire:

1. They charge too much.
2. I cannot understand what they actually charge.
3. They are always trying to sell me a "company" product.
4. They are overly aggressive in recommendations.
5. They constantly change my investments
6. The investment strategy is too complicated.
7. Nobody listens to my opinion.
8. My calls are secondary to the richer guy's.
9. Nobody will take ownership of mistakes.
10. Investments have poor returns.

Not surprisingly, a do-it-yourself investment approach addresses many of the shortcomings of financial experts.

Financial advisors are ubiquitous in the United States, where many investors hire them to assist with investing, financial planning, and other types of financial decision-making. Advisors can be helpful when people lack the expertise or the time to devote to addressing esoteric or complex financial questions. If you seek advice in areas where information is ambiguous, however, and it's hard to judge the quality of the advice based on your own knowledge, you can get stuck with a second-order problem:

What is your basis for relying on the advisor in the first place?

Especially under conditions of uncertainty, what gives you confidence that you should trust the advisor and that the advice is any good? As we discussed in Part One of this book, there are many reasons why we shouldn't put faith in an expert.

Periodically, it comes time to review these relationships. So how do people assess the quality of advice they get from their advisors?

Should You Trust Your Advisor?

Certainly, you can consider an advisor's decision-making track record. How good has the advice been in the past? For example, do you get a monthly statement comparing your returns to a benchmark? Has following the advice led to good outcomes? But this hindsight approach has its challenges.

Some decisions are rare. A home mortgage, for instance, a change in marital status, a windfall, or selection of a fund for a retirement account, may be one-time events, where it may take many years to see whether the advice was good. Additionally, adverse economic shocks, like the financial crisis, or idiosyncratic risks, like a huge drawdown in, say, a gold position, may also cloud your ability to judge the quality of the advice. So you may have to fall back on other means to draw your conclusions.

Perhaps the advisor has similar values to yours. They exhibit a lot of professionalism. These presumably have something to do with their ability to provide advice, don't they? More generally, the most fundamental question one must answer is do you *trust* the advisor? Of course, as the great Ernest Hemingway quipped, "The best way to find out if you can trust somebody is to trust them." But now we are faced with a chicken-and-egg problem. On the one hand, we want to work with someone trustworthy, but on the other hand, maybe we need to work with someone first to ascertain if they are trustworthy. What should we do?

We're not sure we agree with Mr. Hemingway, at least in this context. Blindly following someone's advice and then evaluating them after the fact might not be an ideal approach, but is one that many follow. Identifying who is trustworthy, without having worked with them before, is a highly subjective activity that allows experts an opportunity to exploit our vulnerabilities. And even if we have worked with them before, establishing trust in them is sometimes simply a matter of feelings or personal opinion. Yet as we move from observing tangible, performance-related outcomes, to more subjective approaches involving "trust," we can get into trouble. The problem is that we sometimes trust advisors based on criteria that have nothing to do with their competence. Our trust can be misplaced. That is, we may consider an advisor to be trustworthy, and thereby view the person with approval, when in fact we are getting bad advice. As it turns out, this happens all the time.

In *Individual Judgment and Trust Formation: An Experimental Investigation of Online Financial Advice*, a working paper by Julie R. Agnew et al., the authors explore how trust is related to the assessment of advisor performance. The research highlights some surprising factors that influence our evaluations of an advisor's quality. In what should not be a surprise at this point, many individuals' evaluation metrics are entirely unrelated to the quality of advice given. As a side note, while the research was conducted in Australia, we have few doubts that it reflects realities here in the United States as well.

Should We Really Trust Anyone?

The paper illuminates many of the factors that lead people to trust advisors. For instance, the authors find that people prefer younger advisors. Is this a reliable criterion for assessing trustworthiness? They also prefer people who have professional certifications. However, given the blizzard of existing certifications in the United States, understanding which credentials matter is nontrivial. People also are "sticky" with their advisors, perhaps exhibiting a form of endowment effect or familiarity bias, in which we underestimate the riskiness of something simply because we are familiar with it. Just because you've been with an advisor for 20 years does not mean you are getting good advice. And yet, this is exactly what many believe.

These factors may have little or nothing to do with providing good financial advice, *and yet we rely on them*. Ambiguous situations give rise to additional opportunities for the clever advisor to game the system, and manipulate and exploit clients. For instance, the paper describes the psychological ploy of *catering*, which occurs when an advisor agrees with an investor's suggested approach to gain trust. Once trust is established, they can then disagree with the approach and offer bad advice.

A particularly interesting finding was that people were heavily affected by advice related to easy financial topics, offered early on in an advisory relationship. The paper describes an experiment in which advisors gave advice on "easy" topics, as well as on "hard" topics. The researchers find that if an adviser gives correct advice on an "easy" topic, the respondent can judge the quality easily, allowing them to form a firm opinion of the adviser. However, if this same adviser then follows with advice on a "hard" topic, judging the advice quality is difficult and the respondent starts making bad decisions. The respondent, who really can't judge the advice on the "hard" topic, relies on their prior judgement of the "easy" advice to determine if the "hard" topic advice is good or bad. As a result, a pre-existing good opinion of the adviser will be reinforced by "ambiguous" advice on a hard topic, regardless of whether the advice is really correct or not. This explains why advisers who can establish their trustworthiness early on in a relationship continue to be trusted, even if they give the wrong advice on hard topics.

The research on trust and relationships is scary. People can naively trust people in fancy suits bearing advice on simple financial matters. As the research shows, all you need to do is show some familiarity with the simple stuff. If the investor trusts you based on the simple advice, you can say whatever you want about the hard stuff!

An example illustrates how this might work in practice. Consider two scenarios:

Easy Scenario

Advisor: "You have credit card debt and a large cash position. The interest you're earning on the cash is less than the interest expense on the credit card debt. You should pay off your credit card debt."

Hard Scenario

Advisor: "So you're interested in investing in an index fund? All these funds will match the index returns, but some have been around for a long time and have managers who have established a reputation in the industry, and that kind of quality is really important for any investment product. You should be skeptical of funds with the lowest management fees, since these are going to be funds you've never heard of, with managers who aren't well established."

What's that, you say? This example is unrealistic? Think no financial advisor would ever give advice this obviously bad?

Consider the MainStay S&P 500 Index Fund Class A mutual fund (ticker: MSXAX), for which the expense ratio is 60 basis points (as well as a 3 percent front-end load). Let's look at Morningstar's analysis of the past 10 years of its performance versus its index, the S&P 500 total return index, shown in Table 5.1.

As you would expect, the MSXAX trails its benchmark by the margin of its expense ratio (60 basis points). Now, why would you invest in this fund, when you can invest in a tax-efficient ETF index for essentially nothing? We can't really think of a good reason. In fact, we can't think of a reason why this fund should even exist—*but the fund manages over $2 billion!* It stands to reason that some financial advisor, somewhere,

TABLE 5.1 MainStay S&P 500 Index Fund Performance as of December 5, 2014

MSXAX Performance	YTD	1 Yr.	3 Yr.	5 Yr.	10 Yr.
Fund	13.81	18.00	20.06	15.16	7.33
S&P 500 TR USD	14.45	18.67	20.76	15.83	7.95
+/− S&P 500 TR USD	−0.64	−0.67	−0.70	−0.67	−0.61

somehow, must be recommending it. And if so, this strikes us as objectively bad advice.

While an index fund is a fairly straightforward example for many, it illustrates the point that there are investors out there who are not thinking about index investing in the right way. And so what happens when we move on to additional "hard" areas in finance? Questions about diversification, asset allocation, risk management, exotic hedge fund strategies, and so on; how do we assess decisions made by advisors in these areas? What about our favorite complicated subject—taxes? The same concept applies. Just because an advisor can give you good advice on "easy" topics does not mean you should necessarily rely on advice in other areas.

Various studies have shown that we systematically overestimate the quality of advice we receive. For example, the working paper referenced above describes how the financial services regulator in Australia undertook a study of how consumers perceived the quality of advice they were getting. They evaluated the objective quality of advice given to a small sample of Australians seeking retirement advice. They found only 3 percent of the advice could be considered good quality, while the majority of the advice (58 percent) was adequate and the remaining advice was poor. Despite these low evaluations from the Australian regulator, most participants (86 percent) ranked the quality of the advice they were receiving as "high." In addition, 81 percent trusted the advice they received from their advisor "a lot." This simple study suggests that people can have difficulty objectively assessing the quality of advice given. And why should we expect they could accurately assess such advice? The investing skills they lack, which are why they are seeking advice in the first place, are the same skills they would need to differentiate good from bad advice. Often, what we perceive as high-quality advice is, in fact, terrible advice.

At the end of the day, a trustworthy and competent financial advisor can be an exceptional ally for a struggling investor. But how we find these wonderful advisors is a challenge: It is difficult to assess the quality of advisors and their financial advice. As consumers of financial advice, we can at least be aware of common behavioral pitfalls to which we may be vulnerable. We should also be aware that much of the advice from financial experts is poisoned with bias and overconfidence. All of this suggests that managing our own portfolios is not such a radical concept.

THE FACTS FRAMEWORK

If we can't trust advisors, on average, and we can't trust ourselves because of our innate bias, who can we trust? Not surprisingly, we suggest that investors stick to a systematic framework to assess investment opportunities. Our framework is called the FACTS, which is a mnemonic acronym we will explain shortly. And while there is no "one-size fits all" strategy assessment and allocation model, a systematic framework for decision-making can help simplify the process and maximize returns.

For every investment strategy that needs to be assessed, the FACTS framework (consisting of Fees, Access, Complexity, Taxes, and Search) can be employed to clarify important considerations for the prospective investor. Our experience suggests that the vast majority of taxable family offices and high-net-worth individuals should focus on strategies with lower costs, higher accessibility and liquidity, easily understood investment processes, higher tax-efficiency, and limited due diligence requirements. For example, the FACTS would suggest, in general, that investors make use of more managed accounts and low-cost passively managed 1940 Act products (ETFs and mutual funds), and fewer private hedge funds and private equity vehicles. Using the FACTS framework can help assess cost/benefit trade-offs across strategy characteristics, which, in turn, improves portfolio results net of taxes, fees, and overall brain damage.

F: Fees

"I can't figure out why anyone invests in active management, so asking me about hedge funds is just an extreme version of the same question."
　　　　—Eugene Fama, at the Investment Management Consultants
　　　　　　　　　　　　　　　Association 2013 Conference

Traditional "two and twenty" hedge fund compensation, referring to fees of 2 percent on assets and 20 percent of the gains, has been an industry standard for years. These days, 2/20 has been reduced to something more like 1/20, and with an ounce of negotiation, fees may drop to 1/10. To ascertain where fees have been and where they might be going, we highlight some tables from Ken French's work on the "Cost of Active Investing."[1] Table 5.2 shows the time series of expenses charged by mutual funds from 1980 through 2006 (CEF stands for closed-end fund). All-in expense ratios went from over 200bps to around 100bps.

Table 5.3 highlights hedge fund fees from 1996 to 2007. As compared with mutual fund fees, hedge fund fees have stayed fairly steady over time. Although hedge fund fees still have room to fall, and mutual fund fees represent a step in the right direction, with serious negotiation and persistence, it may be increasingly the case that fees can be "whatever you think is fair,

TABLE 5.2 Fund Fees over Time (1980 to 2006)

	Open-end Mutual Funds				Expense Ratio	
	Expense Ratio	Annuitized Load	Total	Percent Passive	CEFs	ETFs
1980	70	149	219			
1981	71	167	237			
1982	75	128	203			
1983	76	113	190			
1984	82	114	196	1.0		
1985	80	105	185	1.1		
1986	81	101	183	0.8		
1987	86	96	182	0.9		
1988	96	97	193	1.2		
1989	94	84	178	1.6		
1990	93	76	169	2.3		
1991	90	65	155	2.9		
1992	96	50	146	3.9		
1993	98	47	145	3.9		
1994	98	42	139	4.7		
1995	96	42	139	4.7		
1996	93	40	134	5.8		
1997	92	35	126	7.3		
1998	90	30	120	9.0		
1999	91	27	117	9.7		
2000	96	24	119	9.8	96	
2001	97	19	116	10.9	92	20
2002	98	18	116	12.9	101	17
2003	96	17	113	12.4	98	18
2004	91	18	108	12.7	104	19
2005	87	16	103	12.5	103	20
2006	85	15	100	12.6	109	21

since we'd love an allocation." Certainly we would advocate for negotiating fees lower generally, but in addition, investors can apply the FACTS to give them context for thinking about these fees.

A steady reduction in fees is becoming the new norm for the investment management industry. Lower fees are a good thing for investors, less so for investment managers. Yet, the achievement of low fees, per se, is not a panacea for the investor; the appropriate level of manager compensation depends on the situation. For instance, international markets are inherently more expensive to trade than domestic markets due to the high costs of maintaining overseas brokerage and custody operations. Another example might be a highly active strategy with high expected performance that is

TABLE 5.3 Hedge Fund Fees over Time (1996 to 2007)

| | | US Equity-related Hedge Funds | | |
| | | Performance Fee | | Total |
	Mgmt. Fee	Quoted Performance Fee	Realized Performance Fee	Mgmt. Fee + Realized Performance Fee
1996	0.92	18.24	3.79	4.71
1997	1.05	18.4	5.4	6.45
1998	0.98	18.25	2.56	3.54
1999	1.03	18.24	5.91	6.94
2000	1.09	18.42	2.35	3.44
2001	1.2	18.93	1.51	2.71
2002	1.24	19.09	1.38	2.62
2003	1.25	19.12	3.4	4.65
2004	1.23	19.03	2.28	3.51
2005	1.26	19.03	2.18	3.44
2006	1.27	18.95	3.25	4.52
2007	1.28	19.15	3.35	4.63

not available elsewhere in the marketplace and that cannot be replicated at a lower cost. Nonetheless, leaving such nuances aside, here are some basic questions one must ponder when thinking about fees.

What Are the Effective All-in Fees? Here are some questions you might want to ask. Who pays for service providers? What about compensation using so-called soft dollars, or the manager's ability to push operating costs onto the investors? Does the strategy push the client into a higher-price commission regime so the manager can benefit? How about other trading and execution costs? Is order flow being sold to a third party? Are there any 12b-1 fees? What about fund administration, fund accounting, or board fees for mutual funds? Are there any out-of-pocket reimbursements? How is performance calculated when an investor withdraws, in whole or in part? Are there withdrawal penalties? Any discretionary mark-to-market accounting or suspect third-party valuations? Beware of the fine print! Remember that fees compound over time, so scrutinize them carefully.

Do Fees Align Investor and Manager Incentives? Charging a performance fee can make sense, but is there a clawback provision if the manager loses all your money after a great year? What is the hurdle? For example, a 0 percent hurdle for a product with generic market exposure doesn't make sense, because an investor can buy market exposure for next to nothing!

Why should you pay more simply because the market happened to go up? Is there a high-water mark provision? Do managers "eat their own cooking," and invest in their own funds, which can align incentives and address conflicts of interest? If a manager doesn't own what he recommends you should own, think twice about placing your own money with the manager.

What Are the Alternatives?   Many funds are "closet" indexers. Can we clone the manager's exposure via relatively low-cost financial engineering? In other words, is my long/short equity manager more than 95 percent correlated with a strategy that simply goes long the Russell 2000 Value Index and short the S&P 500 index? If a cloning technology costs 50 bps and gets 95 percent of the exposure, the manager needs to either: (1) drop his fees; or (2) not get an allocation. So-called *smart beta* products are another area where investors can often reproduce smart beta exposure, but more cheaply, by financial engineering smart beta products into their constituent components.

A: Access

> "The possibility that liquidity might disappear from a market, and so not be available when it is needed, is a big source of risk to an investor."
> —*The Economist*, September 23, 1999[2]

In *The Wizard of Oz*, Dorothy's traveling party sings, "Lions, and tigers, and bears, oh my!" But in the investment management world, it's more like, "Lock-ups, gates, and redemption fees, oh my!" Dorothy and her friends would be justifiably terrified of today's managers and the many access-reducing strategies they employ. If there exists a way for a manager to maintain a positive lock on your capital, you can bet he will be happy to attempt it. Nonetheless, maintaining flexibility and access to one's capital is critical in an uncertain world where unforeseen liquidity needs may occur, opportunities can arise unexpectedly, and managers can go from "hero" to "zero" in the blink of an eye. In some specialized situations, giving up access might make sense, but all too often investors do not fully assess the cost/benefit of access. It should be noted that most mutual funds and ETFs do not have restrictions on capital; however, some do, so keep reading even if you never plan to invest in a hedge fund or private equity.

The empirical evidence on investor access suggests there is a wide range of access provisions in the marketplace.[3] Access rights are especially important in private vehicles, such as real estate funds, hedge funds, or private equity funds. George Aragon analyzes a database of hedge funds and reveals

TABLE 5.4 Hedge Fund Lockup Periods

Lockup (months)	0	1	3	6	9	12	18	22	24	30	90
Fund	2,380	15	15	38	1	404	1	1	12	3	1

some surprising results. In Table 5.4, Aragon highlights that over 16 percent of hedge funds lock up investor capital in the fund for one year or longer.

Does this make sense?

Perhaps, but here are some questions to consider.

How Can I Access My Capital? Monthly redemption with 90-day notice and a promise to send funds within 90 days of liquidation is really six-month+ redemption. There can be side pockets, notice requirements, redemption suspensions, and other provisions that limit, or restrict, redemption rights. And if you don't know what these terms are, be wary of such investments— make sure you know what you are buying! Watch for semantic shenanigans in subscription agreements. The devil is in the details.

What Is the Underlying Liquidity of the Assets? Do the access privileges line up with the liquidity of the underlying assets? Monthly liquidity for a manager trading illiquid pink-sheets, or five-year locks for a manager trading mega-caps, probably don't make sense. The former may subject you to drawdowns during redemptions, while the latter is simply unjustifiable. Be on the lookout for mismatches between portfolio asset liquidity and portfolio manager liquidity provisions. There are other hazards, including in-kind distributions and preferential liquidity rights.

What Is My Investment Vehicle? Limited partnerships are theoretically interesting, but what happens when another LP sues the fund and everyone's capital is locked up? Also, consider that, technically, a general partner of an LP can have access to client funds (think Bernie Madoff). Go for separately managed accounts (SMAs) or an exchange-traded fund (ETF) vehicle, when possible. These vehicles ensure your capital is available when you want it. That way, you can go to cash and wire the proceeds to a bank account on the same day, if you like.

Does It Reduce My Ability to Tactically Allocate Assets? After dropping 20 percent of your capital into private equity, venture capital, and hedge funds, all with five-year+ lockups, you suddenly realize that the markets have blown up and your "alternatives" exposure is now 60 percent of your capital—you'd love to scale back, and perhaps reallocate to areas where dislocations have created opportunity in liquid markets, but you *cannot.* Yikes. Illiquid alternatives can have dramatic effects on overall allocation flexibility in adverse markets.

C: Complexity

> "Any intelligent fool can make things bigger, more complex, and more violent. It takes a touch of genius, and a lot of courage, to move in the opposite direction."
>
> —E.F. Schumacher

Jason Zweig's book, *Your Money and Your Brain*, highlights an interesting conversation with Harry Markowitz, who won a Nobel Prize in 1990 for his groundbreaking work in portfolio selection. In their conversation, Zweig asks Markowitz how he invests his own money. Markowitz responds with the following:

> *"I should have computed the historical covariance of the asset classes and drawn an efficient frontier ... I split my contributions 50/50 between bonds and equities."*[4]

The intellectual leader behind modern portfolio management is an equal-weight asset allocator? We'll come back to the quote in a moment, but first let's review some general observations on Markowitz's mathematically sophisticated approach to asset allocation—the one he chose to disregard when it came to his own portfolio.

The mean-variance story is compelling. Mean-variance optimization involves calculating the returns of each asset and correlations for each pair of assets, and solving for the efficient frontier that maximizes returns while minimizing risk. It's an approach that would make any math teacher smile. But there is an important assumption embedded in the approach: the inputs, which are based on history, amount to a forecast of returns, correlations, and volatility for the future.

Although Markowitz did win a Nobel Prize, at least partly based on his elegant mathematical solution to identifying mean-variance efficient portfolios, a funny thing happened when his ideas were applied in the real world: mean-variance performed poorly.

The reason is that the *historical* returns, and correlations, which informed the input for the optimization algorithm, were *different* from what investors actually experienced in the real world in the future. That is, the estimates were "unstable," in the sense that they turned out to be guesses that simply weren't any good.

Academics began to see the basic flaw in the approach: Estimates for any covariance matrix are going to be unstable, and thus the "optimized" weights spit out from a model influenced by an unstable covariance matrix will also end up being unstable and unreliable. And so this highly engineered, mathematically beautiful, and Nobel Prize–winning approach translated into a no-value-added-situation for investors.

This is something to keep in mind when considering any optimization method for asset allocation. It also emphasizes a critical point related to asset allocation that every investor should be aware of: *Complexity does not equal value.*

Recall Charlie Munger's admonition to "invert, always invert." So if complexity does not equal value, is it perhaps simplicity that equals value? Later in Chapter 6, we will discuss how simple equal-weight allocations do indeed seem to reliably beat complex allocation approaches.

Markowitz himself may have realized the value of simplicity intuitively. Consider the irony: The founder of modern portfolio theory uses an equal-weight allocation. And one of the central assumptions underlying mean-variance optimization is that investors care about risk and return trade-offs. Yet, as Markowitz highlights, his decision-making framework has little to do with risk and return trade-offs. In 2014, now that we have a long enough data trail, we can show that Markowitz's model doesn't outperform a simple equal-weight allocation. The reason for this under-performance is not a critique of the model, which is clearly an incredible intellectual achievement, but has everything to do with the practical realities of accurately estimating a covariance matrix. We will come back to this issue later in the chapter and in the next, when we explore asset allocation in more detail.

The point, however, is that academic insights and good models don't necessary translate into good practical ideas. This insight is helpful for a do-it-yourself investor, because it implies that we don't need a PhD in finance to implement a reasonable asset-allocation strategy.

Why Does This Strategy Need to Be Complex? Is the complexity a front for the manager, or does the complexity of the strategy drive the alpha? There is seldom a connection between a strategy's complexity and its effectiveness. If you are having trouble understanding why the complexity exists, it may be intentional on the part of the manager. If the manager cannot justify the complexity relative to a simpler model than the complexity is not necessary.

How Robust Is the System? Complexity is often correlated with data fitting, for example, when managers identify a very specific allocation scheme that has worked in a small sample. If the complex system is slightly changed, do results completely dry up? If they do, then the system is not robust. Reversion to the mean, and mediocre performance, or much worse, is in your future.

Can You Explain the Strategy to Stakeholders? Clarity and simplicity help facilitate communication and education, which breeds trust and confidence. Outsourcing investment activity to managers with highly complex, expensive, and opaque investment strategies does not facilitate clear communication. And while it might not matter if the portfolio is making money, what happens when it starts losing? Suddenly, understanding becomes very important, as people start asking difficult questions. Defending a losing investment in a Vanguard index fund is easier than defending a loss in credit default swaps.

Risk Management? Any banker who lived through the 2008 financial crisis understands how complication can create risk-management problems. How does one risk manage a machine-learning algorithm that is trading leveraged exotic derivatives with a jump-diffusion model, infused with a touch of fractal mathematics and string theory? Black boxes of this sort can be problematic for risk managers. In short, always ask yourself if the complexity of a strategy creates a risk management blind spot.

T: Taxes

> "Another very simple effect I very seldom see discussed either by investment managers or anybody else is the effect of taxes … If you sit back for long, long stretches in great companies, you can get a huge edge from nothing but the way that income taxes work."
> —Charlie Munger, *On the Art of Stock Picking*

Tax minimization strategies are—and always will be—a critical aspect of long-term wealth creation. Tax efficiency is an important investment consideration that is often overlooked, even by experienced allocators. Indeed, tax considerations often predominate over performance considerations. This cruel investment calculus often seems lost on mutual fund investors. Over long periods of time, a tax drag of 50 percent or more a year on a short-term trading strategy has a tough time outlasting an inferior investment strategy that defers taxes for many years into the future.

Some scary numbers: Starting in 2013, the marginal investor will pay 23.8 percent on long-term capital gains (20 percent plus 3.8 percent health care tax) and 43.4 percent (39.6 percent plus 3.8 percent health-care tax)

TABLE 5.5   Tax Rate Increases from 2012 to 2013

	2012 Tax Rate	2013 Tax Rate	Health Care Tax	2013 Total	% Increase
Tax-exempt Interest	0%	0%	0%	0%	0%
Qualified Dividends	15%	20%	4%	24%	59%
Long-term Gains	15%	20%	4%	24%	59%
Nonqualified Dividends	35%	40%	4%	43%	24%
Short-term Gains	35%	40%	4%	43%	24%
Taxable Interest	35%	40%	4%	43%	24%

Source: Internal Revenue Service Documents.

on short-term capital gains (see Table 5.5). These figures do not include city, state, or local taxes, which can boost these figures much higher (e.g., California) (see Table 5.5).

The tax bite matters: Consider a manager returning 30 percent a year. Yes, it's an amazing return, but the manager churns the portfolio consistently to generate these returns. After a 43.4 percent tax, this yields only 16.98 percent to his investors. Another manager makes 22.28 percent a year—quite an accomplishment—but this manager trades less frequently to lock in long-term capital gains. After tax, this managers' return is 16.98 percent. Finally, consider a buy and hold manager that generates 16.98 percent a year, but never sells or rebalances the portfolio. After tax, this manager still makes 16.98 percent. All three managers generate 16.98 percent after-tax returns, but the three managers have very different pretax results, and therefore offer vastly different security-selection skill levels. But that doesn't matter. In these cases, alpha is irrelevant—it is tax efficiency that matters.

Consider the following when it comes to taxes.

Tax Efficiency? How are returns taxed? Can this strategy be more tax-efficient? Why or why not? Can it ever be tax-efficient?

Tax Externalities? For any actively managed equity strategies, avoid mutual funds. These vehicles generate 1099s with unpredictable tax liabilities. Avoid limited partnership hedge fund structures with hidden "basis." Investing is tough enough—avoid embedded tax liabilities at all costs.

Does the Alpha Justify the Tax Costs? Alpha of 5 percent a year, with a 10 percent tax drag, nets out to a −5 percent liability. Not good. A good question to ask is what your after-tax alpha would have been when viewing a great backtest.

Tax Risks? Maybe this strategy is too aggressive. Are the tax benefits of this strategy too good to be true? Are the managers "pushing the envelope" with untested tax approaches? Could it trigger an unwanted audit? Are there tax and legislative risks that can be assessed? IRS rules can change; lawsuits can occur; lawyers are expensive, and you need to pay them with after-tax dollars.

S: Search

> "There are about 8,000 planes in the air and 100 really good pilots."
> —Ray Dalio in 2020 Vision

We've finally got the report from our consultant telling us that we need 40 percent of our assets in hedge funds. Great, let's go hire the best hedge fund managers! Wait a second, now we have to compile a list of candidates, fly around the world interviewing people, conduct due diligence, and after all that maybe we need to hire yet another consultant who specializes in understanding hedge fund strategies. Suddenly, manager search isn't as easy as we previously expected. How can we be confident in our ability to identify the very best? Even once we have the managers, things don't get easier. We have to monitor them each year, do on-site visits, watch for style drift, make sure their growth will not impact their returns, etc. Search costs are a real cost associated with particular portfolio allocations. One needs to weigh the benefits of more exotic allocations, such as hedge funds, private equity, and venture capital, against these costs. Different questions to address regarding search costs:

How Will I Identify Managers? If we lower portfolio risk via an exotic allocation, but incur an annualized 200bps in search costs to attain the allocation, does it still make sense?

How Will I Monitor Managers? Compared to a 1940 Act product, exotic allocations require more hands-on monitoring and periodic reassessment. Now we need a staff with specialized expertise. Or maybe we outsource to a consultant. How much is this going to cost?

How Will I Deal with Manager Turnover? As a one-time expense, manager search costs might not be too prohibitive. However, consider the fact that managers can fail or leave the business, and the need to maintain a stable of the top managers is an on-going process. Additionally, there can be significant switching costs associated with moving to new managers, including commissions, market impact, and the opportunity costs of being out of the market during a transition.

FACTS Conclusion

Staring at performance charts is only the first step when deciding on an investment strategy. A range of additional factors must be considered. The world is infinitely complicated, and these factors need to be assessed critically and individually when investing. The FACTS framework can help identify the right questions, which will help investors make better decisions. The FACTS framework consists of Fees, Access, Complexity, Taxes, and Search. By no means does the FACTS framework cover every aspect of strategy selection or investment decision-making, but we hope it will provide an important tool for investors as they seek to deploy their hard-earned capital most effectively.

WE'VE GOT THE FACTS: NOW WHAT?

We have established some FACTS to consider using the framework just outlined. Where do we go from here? Next, we outline the building blocks of portfolio management, which consist of the following three concepts:

1. Asset Allocation
2. Risk Management
3. Security Selection

Asset Allocation

The father of modern portfolio theory, whom we alluded to earlier in this chapter, was Harry Markowitz, who developed techniques to maximize returns while minimizing risk through portfolio diversification (he won a Nobel Prize for his work in 1990). Modern portfolio theory, as formulated by Markowitz, states that investors should seek to maximize expected returns while minimizing the expected variance of those returns (the tangency portfolio described above). This is achieved through diversification, since investing in asset classes with low covariance results in a lower overall portfolio variance than investing in individual asset classes. Markowitz's ideas have been extensively developed within academia and the world of finance over the past 50 years.

We begin the portfolio investing process by identifying the basic building blocks which can provide diversification. We divide asset classes into three broad categories: (1) equities, (2) real assets, and (3) fixed income investments.

Equities are ownership interests in operating businesses, and provide exposure to earnings growth and dividend income. Real assets are tangible, physical assets whose intrinsic value is related to their utility, which enables them to be exchanged for other products or services. These are real estate and commodities. Real assets may generate cash flow, and have traditionally been viewed as a means of providing protection against inflation. Fixed income relates to investments that generate a return based on stable periodic payments at regular intervals with a return of principal at maturity. Fixed income investments, or bonds, typically provide income and have low historical volatility.

Asset Allocation—Flaws in Mean-Variance Optimization? While Markowitz's pioneering research in the 1950s highlighted the benefits of diversifying across multiple asset classes, there has been substantial debate over the ensuing decades on the best way to achieve this. Since investors can generate varying rates of return and assume alternative levels of risk by combining quantities of asset classes in different ways, this debate has focused on the development of theoretical models that have provided insight into an array of weighting methodologies.

These methodologies have offered competing approaches to optimizing portfolio performance over time, but they are all based on attempts to simultaneously maximize return while assuming the least amount of risk, also referred to as *mean-variance optimization.*

Despite the diversity and sophistication of these models, there are two criticisms common to all of them: (1) the length of the sample periods tested, which are short, and (2) the estimates of return and volatility used to calculate the allocation rules, which can change in the future. Fundamentally, these models are derived from uniformly small samples whose results often do not hold up when implemented over long, out-of-sample, time frames, and their return and volatility estimates, also when applied out-of-sample, tend to be noisy and prone to error over time, which often results in the models' diverging, sometimes radically, from predicted outcomes.

As it turns out, this problem is not unique to financial markets.

As Daniel Kahneman points out in his 2011 book, *Thinking Fast and Slow:*

> *... The dominant statistical practice in the social sciences is to assign weights to the different predictors by following an algorithm, called multiple regression ... The logic of multiple regression is unassailable: it finds the optimal formula for putting together a weighted combination of the predictors ... One can do just as well by selecting a set of scores that have some validity for predicting the outcomes and adjusting the values to make them comparable (by using standard scores or ranks). A formula that combines these predictors with equal weights is likely to be just as accurate in predicting new cases*

as the multiple-regression formula that was optimal in the original sample ... The important conclusion ... is that an algorithm that is constructed on the back of an envelope is often good enough to compete with an optimally weighted formula.[5]

Is it possible that a simplified weighting regime for asset classes will offer performance comparable, or perhaps superior to, the rich body of portfolio research that has emerged over the past half century? We explore this question in Chapter 6.

Risk Management

In general, while efforts to time the market should be viewed with skepticism, certain risk-management, or "market-timing" strategies, which have been explored in academia, appear to reduce risk, without significantly impacting long-run returns. In particular, the application of simple moving average rules has been demonstrated to protect investors from large market drawdowns, which is defined as the peak-to-trough decline experienced by an investor.

Jeremy Siegel, in his book, *Stocks for the Long Run*, explores the effect on performance on the Dow Jones Industrial Average from 1886 to 2006, when applying a 200-day moving average rule. Siegel found that this simple technical rule outperforms a buy-and-hold approach, both in absolute terms and on a risk-adjusted basis.[6]

This simple strategy seems to protect investors from large drawdowns, which are difficult to recover from. Research indicates that the rule can be used effectively across asset classes. We will explore more ideas and concepts in Chapter 7.

Security Selection

There are literally hundreds of academic papers written on "anomalies," or strategies that purport to beat the market on a risk-adjusted basis. Anomaly chasing has become so popular that academics have written papers making fun of other academics. John Cochrane calls the literature on anomalies a "zoo of new factors."[7] For example, Harvey Campbell, Yan Liu, and Heqing Zhu examine 316 papers that study seemingly anomalous patterns published in a selection of academic journals. The authors highlight that there is a bias toward publishing findings that have strong statistical significance, but disregard (1) that some of these may be empirical tests unrelated to any theory and thus possibly data mined, and (2) in finance, unlike in science, no one publishes replication studies, and so there is little verification of discovered factors. Campbell et al. argue "that most claimed research findings in financial economics are likely false."[8] The authors also find that there are some anomalies that still appear anomalous, even after accounting for data-snooping. Of all the anomalies documented in academic literature, the two most durable strategies identified are value and momentum strategies.

Value Strategies The value investing philosophy, established by Benjamin Graham in the 1930s, is based on buying securities at prices that are low relative to their intrinsic value. While Graham intuitively grasped the effectiveness of buying stocks at low prices, academics began to explore the concept with rigorous analysis, beginning in the 1970s, with some noting that portfolios constructed with firms with high earnings-to-price or book-to-market ratios, high dividend yields, or a high ratio of cash flow to price seemed to earn abnormal returns above what was expected. In the 1990s, Eugene Fama and Kenneth French famously identified the *value premium*, and demonstrated that value stocks have delivered higher returns with lower volatility over long periods of time.[9] A growing body of work further refined the *value anomaly*, which today is among most firmly established effects in financial markets. More recently, academics have begun to explore how the value anomaly can be applied to additional asset classes beyond equities. There are a number of academic papers and studies describing how investors can apply the value investing approach in new and creative ways.[10]

Researchers have also begun to explore the question of why these strategies produce superior returns. Today, some of the literature suggests that innate human behavioral bias plays a role in the value effect, as investors overreact to stocks or assets that have performed poorly and, underestimating their future growth prospects, oversell them. We suggest that investors should seek out approaches to exploiting the value anomaly across various asset classes, and in particular the benefits of individual security selection available within equity markets.

Momentum Strategies Momentum in finance refers to the tendency of investments that have done well in the recent past to continue doing well, and of investments that have done poorly to continue doing poorly. As with value, the concept of momentum in securities markets has been around a long time. As far back as the 1920s, famed stock picker Jessie Livermore, immortalized in the book *Reminiscences of a Stock Operator*, was using momentum-like strategies to beat the market. With the passage of time, academics inevitably began to study the effect in earnest, beginning in roughly the 1990s, and hundreds of papers on the subject have since appeared in the literature.

Recently, Christopher Geczy and Mikhail Samanov explored the momentum effect extensively over a long time frame, in their paper *212 Years of Price Momentum (The World's Longest Backtest: 1801–2012)*, which clearly establishes and documents the persistence of momentum over two full centuries in US equity markets.[11] Academics have now established that momentum works across a range of asset classes, and in markets outside of the United States.

Once again, as with value, it appears that innate human behavioral bias may explain the existence of the effect. New research is exploring specific behavioral traits that give rise to the momentum effect, including how investors are slow to incorporate news into their forecasts, and use recent performance of securities as a signal. We investigate value and momentum in Chapter 8.

SUMMARY

Chapter 5 questions the trust we put in our experts when it comes to investing. We then nudge the reader to consider a do-it-yourself approach. We also reviewed our "FACTS" strategy evaluation framework. Each investment decision should involve a discussion of fees, access, complexity, taxes, and search costs. Finally, we outlined the three core elements of portfolio management: asset allocation, risk-management, and security selection. We explore these three elements in the next three chapters.

NOTES

1. K. French, "The Cost of Active Investing," *Journal of Finance* 63 (2008): 1537–1573.
2. "When the Sea Dries Up," *Economist* (September 23, 2009), http://www .economist.com/node/243068.
3. George O. Aragon, "Share Restrictions and Asset Pricing: Evidence from the Hedge Fund Industry," *Journal of Financial Economics* 83, no. 1 (2007): 33–58.
4. Jason Zweig, *Your Money and Your Brain* (New York: Simon and Schuster, 2008), p. 4.
5. Daniel Kahneman, *Thinking, Fast and Slow* (New York: Macmillan, 2012).
6. Jeremy J. Siegel, *Stocks for the Long Run 5/E: The Definitive Guide to Financial Market Returns & Long-Term Investment Strategies* (New York: McGraw-Hill, 2013).
7. John H. Cochrane, "Presidential Address: Discount Rates," *Journal of Finance* 66 (2011): 1047–1108.
8. H. Campbell, Y. Liu, and H. Zhu, "...and the Cross-Section of Expected Returns," Duke Working Paper (February 3, 2015). http://papers.ssrn.com/sol3/ papers.cfm?abstract_id=2249314.
9. E. F. Fama and K. R. French, "The Cross-Section of Expected Stock Returns," *Journal of Finance* 47, no. 2 (1992): 427–465.
10. C. T. Asness, Moskowitz, and L. Pedersen. "Value and Momentum Everywhere," *Journal of Finance* 68 (2013): 929–985.
11. Christopher C. Geczy, and Mihail Samonov, "212 Years of Price Momentum (The World's Longest Backtest: 1801–2012)" Working paper (August, 2013). http://ssrn.com/abstract=2292544.

CHAPTER 6

A Simple Asset Allocation Model That Works

"Any intelligent fool can make things bigger, more complex, and more violent. It takes a touch of genius—and a lot of courage—to move in the opposite direction."

—Albert Einstein

Einstein is right. In general, complexity implies opacity, and is often a calling card for a manager who is trying to charge excessive fees for a strategy that is easily replicable. One example where we see a healthy dose of complexity in the financial services industry is in asset allocation. The dominant paradigm utilized by massive institutional investors and professional investors is modern portfolio theory, which involves the use of optimization procedures that seek to maximize expected return for a given level of risk. The telltale sign that a manager is using modern portfolio theory is the classic risk/reward graph that shows the "efficient frontier" and the capital allocation line, as set forth in Figure 6.1.

This all sounds great in theory, and Wes and Jack still teach advanced college-level courses on the subject; however, as practitioners and not students-in-training, we are less focused on complex mathematical solutions, and more focused on pragmatic tools that work. We must ask the question, do complex asset-allocation strategies grounded in modern portfolio theory even work? To address this question, we explore a 2009 study by DeMiguel, Garlappi, and Uppal, "Optimal Versus Naïve Diversification," and find something remarkable: a basic equal-weight asset allocation model beats modern portfolio theory and 13 other even more complex strategies.[1] In other words, complexity doesn't add value.

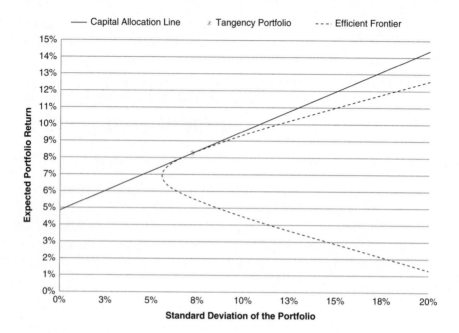

FIGURE 6.1   Classic Modern Portfolio Theory Chart

But how can we make this point more concrete at the outset? Consider an investor who wants to allocate across three asset classes:

1. **Stock Market:** S&P 500
2. **Hedge Funds:** long/short value-focused hedge fund (go long cheap stocks and short expensive stocks)
3. **Fixed Income:** 10-year Treasury bonds

How might such an investor choose to allocate across these three asset classes? Many advisors would recommend mean-variance optimization—the foundation for modern portfolio theory—which involves calculating returns of each asset, and correlations for each pair of assets, and solving for the efficient frontier that maximizes returns while minimizing risk. Remember, the inputs, based on history, translate into a forecast of returns and volatility for the future.

In the following tables, we highlight the fragile nature of complex models like mean-variance-optimization. In Table 6.1, we calculate summary statistics for the S&P 500 total return index (stock market exposure, labeled SP500), the Fama and French long/short value factor (hedge fund exposure, labeled HML), and the 10-year Treasury bond (fixed income exposure,

TABLE 6.1 Summary Statistics

1927–1960	SP500	HML	LTR
Average	1.00%	0.36%	0.26%
Variance	0.005	0.002	0.000
Std. Dev.	7.04%	4.42%	1.26%
Correlation	SP500	HML	LTR
SP500	100.00%	58.93%	5.64%
HML	58.93%	100.00%	4.03%
LTR	5.64%	4.03%	100.00%
1961–2013	SP500	HML	LTR
Average	0.91%	0.40%	0.59%
Variance	0.002	0.001	0.001
Std. Dev.	4.32%	2.83%	2.36%
Correlation	SP500	HML	LTR
SP500	100.00%	−26.41%	16.91%
HML	−26.41%	100.00%	0.44%
LTR	16.91%	0.44%	100.00%

labeled LTR). We calculate monthly returns and related statistics over two subperiods: 1927 to 1960 and from 1961 to 2013. We choose two measurement periods to demonstrate how the choice of look-back period, which informs the input for the optimization algorithm, can drive dramatically different "optimized" allocations. In general, note that averages and standard deviations for these three asset classes don't differ dramatically, but the correlation matrix across the assets shows strong differences, despite being estimated over long time periods.

For many investors, the correlation matrix doesn't factor into asset allocation decisions, but for the herds of professional investors trained in the art of modern portfolio management, correlation matrix estimates matter a great deal. A stable correlation matrix is required if investors want to get reliable estimates for how to make allocations into their portfolio. Yet, as the evidence shows, correlation matrixes, even when calculated based on long time frames, can be highly unstable over discrete periods!

Let's take this concept a step further and look at two ways to create a portfolio using the methods discussed. Table 6.2 shows the recommended portfolio weights using two methods, the tangency portfolio method (maximize risk-adjusted return) and the minimum variance method (minimize risk). Both methods will use our three asset classes: the S&P 500, the

TABLE 6.2 Tangency and Minimum Variance
Portfolio Weights

1927–1960	Tangency Weights	Min. Var. Weights
W(SP500)	17.92%	−0.55%
W(HML)	−5.81%	7.07%
W(LTR)	87.90%	93.48%
1961–2013	Tangency Weights	Min. Var. Weights
W(SP500)	41.22%	18.37%
W(HML)	15.27%	38.95%
W(LTR)	43.51%	42.68%

long/short value hedge fund, and long bonds. The tangency and minimum variance portfolios sound like great ideas: Who doesn't want to maximize risk-adjusted returns or minimize volatility? However, look at the difference in recommended portfolio weights over the two time periods! For the tangency portfolio, from 1927 to 1960, the model recommends an 88 percent allocation to long bonds; however, from 1961 to 2013 the model recommends a 44 percent allocation. Correlation matrices matter!

Remarkably, we find that a simple, equal-weighted allocation outperforms both of these "optimized" portfolios in tests of varying time periods (similar to the results from DeMiguel, Garlappi, and Uppal, 2009). Table 6.3 tabulates the results. The strategies represented are as follows: a strategy that allocates equally to the three asset classes each month (equal weights); a strategy that uses the tangency portfolio weights recommended from 1927 to 1960 (tangency); and a strategy that uses the recommended minimum variance weights estimated from 1927 to 1960 (minimum variance). Since we know that time periods matter, we analyze our results from 1961 to 2013 to *see if the strategy is robust*. We present performance metrics for compound annual growth rates, worst drawdowns, Sharpe ratios, and Sortino ratios (see Table 6.3 for numbers and see the Appendix for the definitions of the various statistics). Based on risk-adjusted metrics, the

TABLE 6.3 Equal-Weight, Tangency, and Minimum-Variance
Performance

1961–2013	Equal Weights	Tangency	Min. Var.
CAGR	7.64%	7.83%	6.81%
Worst Drawdown	−19.90%	−18.14%	−19.90%
Sharpe Ratio	0.73	0.60	0.51
Sortino Ratio	0.64	0.58	0.40

simple equal-weight strategy outperforms the complex asset allocation algorithm (highest Sharpe/Sortino ratios).

What gives?

While mean-variance analysis has reverse engineered the best *historical* Sharpe ratio (i.e., the tangency portfolio), this solution relies on a correlation matrix input, which is highly unstable and incredibly difficult to estimate (most attempts to predict the future are). Consequently, a simple model of $1/N$ beats a more complex model. Moreover, you can be sure that the complex, "proprietary" asset allocation model will have higher fees than a simple $1/N$ approach!

Bankers beware. The data suggest that simple solutions may beat the expensive models when considering asset allocation. Let us now explore a simple asset allocation model that works.

ASSET ALLOCATION

Any investor is undoubtedly familiar with the concept of diversification, the cornerstone of modern portfolio theory. The phrase, "Don't put all of your eggs in one basket," is an old one, but is still familiar in popular culture. Ancient Romans diversified their cargo across several ships, Washington would send important directives via multiple carriers, and we ask our daughters to clean their rooms several times. All these examples have the same mission: Diversify your efforts to increase your chance of success.

When properly diversified, one is not overly concentrated in any particular investment. The diversified investor spreads risk over many different areas, capturing the returns from multiple asset classes while reducing the volatility of the overall nest egg. Cliff Asness calls the benefits of diversification: "the one free lunch of investing." Mr. Asness goes on to say, "When you see a free lunch, the only rational thing to do is eat."[2] We agree, but we need to eat the right lunch and not overindulge. The foundation for capturing the benefits of diversification is not mere diversification, but rather, *intelligent* asset allocation.

In today's sophisticated global financial markets, there are countless possibilities available to the creative investor. From shares in Exxon to Zimbabwean credit markets, Yak futures in Mongolia to Brazilian ore contracts, there's an asset class for any appetite. Perhaps in an ideal world, you might strive for exposure to everything (and what nest egg would be complete without exposure to the Mongolian Yak market)? From a practical standpoint, however, this is impossible. The sheer transaction costs, incremental management fees, and time spent overseeing such a portfolio would be impossible. At some point, we, as diversification enthusiasts, have to make trade-offs.

The question then becomes one related to the FACTS framework outlined earlier: Which asset classes help me achieve my risk/return goals after controlling for Fees, Access, Complexity, Taxes, and Search costs?

For insights into which assets classes may be worth considering for a portfolio, we look to the world of endowment investing and, in particular, to the Yale endowment—the gold standard for institutional investing. Yale's targeted asset classes are broadly broken down into a handful of broad categories (we include Yale's target allocations to each for fiscal 2015):[3]

- Private equity (31%)
- Absolute return (e.g., hedge funds, 20%)
- Real estate (17%)
- Foreign equity (13%)
- Natural resources (8%)
- Domestic equity (6%)
- Bonds and cash (5%)

At first glance, this appears to be a pretty wide-ranging list of asset classes, and in scrutinizing the individual categories, it seems several might be downright unavailable for the average investor. For example, private equity, an asset class famous for high fees, illiquidity, and variable performance, would be pretty tough to implement in our retirement portfolio if we stick to the FACTS. Yale, however, with a dedicated staff, significant negotiating leverage, and decades of experience, can probably pull it off. In fact, private equity is Yale's largest asset allocation! And what about investments in additional esoteric areas—say, timber assets? Investing in tangible natural resources presents numerous challenges for investors like us (unless of course, you manage millions of acres of forest land in your spare time). In short, the complexity of several investments can quickly outweigh their potential return. If you, like Yale, can manage incremental complexity, be sure you are getting the return you deserve.

For the rest of us, we need to rely on more simple approaches. As E. F. Schumacher points out, "Any third-rate engineer or researcher can increase complexity; but it takes a certain flair of real insight to make things simple again."[4] We concur with Schumacher's insight that it is not always easy to make things simpler, especially when it comes to investing. Simplicity requires the discipline of not falling victim to the idea that complexity and activity necessarily add value. Adding bells and whistles is fun, and nobody wants to sit around and "do nothing."

A great example of a simple, do-nothing trade is Van Hoisington's 30-year zero-coupon bond trade—buy-and-hold. Van described his trading activity, or more accurately the lack thereof, at the October 2012 Grant's

Interest Rate Observer Conference, in this way, "I don't do anything and I don't know anything." Van's willingness to do nothing and courage to admit he knows nothing, are two of the greatest traits of the best investors. And while we don't recommend Van's advice, Van has done extremely well with his long-term zero-coupon Treasury bond trade over the past 20-plus years, which highlights that an investor doesn't need to engage in activity to be successful. *Less is sometimes more.*

Similarly, individual investors should accept their own limitations and not feel compelled to invest exactly how Yale invests. Your objectives likely aren't those of Yale's, your tolerance for risk isn't the same, and you probably have a different time horizon. We recommend investors consider a reduced number of asset classes, focusing on those that are easy to manage, easy to invest in, and provide the lion's share of the benefits that accompany a much greater degree of diversification.

In our approach, identify three target assets and map the corresponding allocations from Yale's model into our simple framework. The one asset class we do not cover is the so-called *absolute return* asset class. Roughly translated, this means "expensive, opaque, and tax-inefficient hedge funds," so we exclude this allocation from our opportunity set. The three asset classes are:

- *Equity*: This includes the common stocks of companies:
  - Private, foreign, and domestic equity in the Yale model
- *Bonds*: So-called "risk-free" securities (US government bonds):
  - Bonds and cash in the Yale model
- *Real assets*: Real estate and commodities. Assets are traditionally thought to track inflation growth over time:
  - Real estate and natural resources in the Yale model

Now that we have our three core asset classes, the next step is to determine how to invest. Do we buy individual stocks? A mutual fund? In our view, exchange-traded funds (ETFs), while not a panacea, offer a compelling option. Both cost- and tax-efficient, ETFs are generally the best vehicle for investors and offer the desired exposures to our key asset classes. You can buy exposure at the click of a mouse, and you won't have to choose a hedge fund manager, be stuck in a 10-year private-equity lock-up, or manage a 10,000-acre timber farm.

Thus far, we have limited our discussion to the concept of asset allocation, which is essentially determining the baskets into which you will put your eggs. The next stage of our discussion involves tactics you might employ in your asset allocation process (e.g., how many eggs go into each basket).

If we examine Yale's target allocation percentages for fiscal 2015, we find that they use different weights for each asset class. For example, domestic equities are 6 percent of the target portfolio, while foreign equities are 13 percent. Why the disparity between the levels of exposure? Furthermore, Yale's allocations for 2015 differ from those targeted for 2014. Why the change in allocation targets? These are tactical decisions that reflect perceived opportunities and risks associated with the various asset classes. Yale is constantly tactically reallocating, in order to manage risk and take advantage of prevailing market conditions. So how do they do it?

David Swenson, the chief investment officer for the Yale endowment, has dozens of analysts and economists working for him, as well as many specialized investment companies and third-party advisors all providing him input and perspective on how to allocate. Do you have a similar network to help inform your decision-making? If you're like the vast majority of the investing public, the answer is a resounding "No!" That doesn't mean you can't tactically allocate like the pros, but your approach has to be different, since it cannot involve paying a team of high-priced MBAs to do economic research in your guest bedroom. Your approach needs to be simple, and so we will now describe such a simple approach.

A SIMPLE ASSET ALLOCATION MODEL THAT WORKS

It seems that every financial expert has a long-term asset allocation plan he recommends to the world. Warren Buffett has been quoted as recommending a long-term 90 percent exposure to the S&P 500 and a 10 percent allocation to cash. Jack Bogle, the founder of the Vanguard, suggests a split between the S&P 500 and a bond index. Mr. Buffett and Mr. Bogle are clearly on the left tail of the simplicity distribution, but other market pros have more interesting recommendations. Two prominent examples include David Swensen (Yale CIO), who we have already discussed, and William Bernstein, a prominent author of investing books.

Two Sample Portfolios

Let's look at the two portfolio options posed by our experts:

David Swensen's Portfolio
- David's book, *Unconventional Success*, argues for a simple portfolio consisting of the following: 30 percent domestic equity, 20 percent foreign equity (15 percent developed; 5 percent emerging), 20 percent real estate, 15 percent inflation-protected bonds, and 15 percent in Treasury bonds.[5]

William Bernstein's Portfolio

- William has published numerous books on investing, but in *The Intelligent Asset Allocator,* he argues for a portfolio consisting of the following: 25 percent domestic equity, 25 percent foreign equity, 25 percent small caps, and 25 percent bonds.[6]

These represent the best thinking from respected allocation experts. What other allocations approaches might we consider?

Back in the 1960s and 1970s, a lot of research was conducted to try to assess how pension funds allocated, and it was observed that allocations seemed to coalesce around a simple strategy: 60 percent to domestic equity and 40 percent to bonds. Readers have probably heard of this approach, the "60/40 rule," which is widely perceived as a reasonable asset mix for the long-term investor.

As quant geeks, we naturally want to see what would have happened if we had followed these models over the past 25 years. We conducted an analysis of these different options using the following indices to build Swensen and Bernstein's expert portfolios:

- SP500 = SP500 Total Return Index (domestic equity)
- R2K = Russell 2000 Total Return Index (small cap equity)
- EAFE = MSCI EAFE Total Return Index (developed market equity)
- EEM = MSCI Emerging Markets Total Return Index (emerging market equity)
- REIT = FTSE NAREIT All Equity REITS Total Return Index (real estate)
- GSCI = Goldman Sachs Commodity Index (commodities)
- LTR = Merrill Lynch 7–10 Year Government Bond Index (bonds)
- TIPS = 10-Year Treasury Inflation Protected Securities Index (TIPS)

We conduct our "horserace" from January 1, 1979, through December 31, 2014, as shown in Table 6.4 below. For simplicity, we rebalance on a monthly basis to ensure the portfolios maintain their suggested weights.[7]

Remarkably, the 60/40 portfolio worked the best on a risk-adjusted basis, but overall, each portfolio generated approximately the 10-year Treasury rate over this period (6.53 percent) plus 4 to 5 percent, with about the same volatility. The 60/40 had an easier ride along the way, with a drawdown that is lower than the other options, but for all intents and purposes, we have a three-way tie. Of course, the marginal 60/40 outperformance is driven by the fact that the S&P 500 and 10-year bonds were the top two performing assets over this time period. During a different time period, a more diversified approach is probably a safer bet if one is interested in maximizing

TABLE 6.4 Summary Statistics of Three Strategies

Summary Statistics	60/40	Swensen	Bernstein
CAGR	11.21%	10.62%	11.04%
Standard Deviation	10.07%	10.01%	11.97%
Downside Deviation (MAR = 5%)	6.86%	8.49%	9.26%
Sharpe Ratio	0.64	0.59	0.5
Sortino Ratio (MAR = 5%)	0.90	0.66	0.67
Worst Drawdown	−28.12%	−41.17%	−39.65%
Worst Month Return	−10.79%	−17.07%	−15.21%
Best Month Return	10.05%	11.21%	9.28%
Profitable Months	66.67%	69.21%	66.67%

the benefits of diversification. But the performance of these different strategies is beside the point; *the key insight is that fine-tuning asset-allocation strategies doesn't really matter over long periods.* One can expect to end up in the same spot, on average. This simple study begs the following question.

Does Asset Allocation Even Matter?

We are now wrestling with an uncomfortable prospect (if you are a high-fee-charging advisor): "advanced" asset allocation may be irrelevant. The differences in returns are often noise. Some academics believe that investors only care about the mean and variance of their returns, and thus investors should hold the market portfolio, or the portfolio of _all_ risky assets to diversify as much as possible. Others cling to the tenets of optimizing returns while minimizing risk, and spend countless hours identifying and structuring portfolios that supposedly outperform the market. There are many perturbations of these two schools of thought. But how do the "academic" answers to asset allocation (above) actually stack up against a simple equal-weight strategy?

Victor DeMiguel, Lorenzo Garlappi, and Raman Uppal have a surprising answer to this question in their paper "Optimal Versus Naive Diversification: How Inefficient Is the 1/N Portfolio Strategy?"[8] The authors examine the traditional mean-variance asset allocation approach, but they also examine 12 other complex, sophisticated approaches related to asset allocation. If you are a hardcore quant geek, the specific approaches tested are outlined in Table 6.5. If you are a lay reader, the key takeaway is that this study took the best and brightest asset allocation hypotheses on the planet and compared them to our good old-fashioned 1/N, equal-weight portfolio (again, see Table 6.5).

TABLE 6.5 Asset Allocation Models Tested

# Model	Abbreviation
Naïve	
0. 1/N with rebalancing (*benchmark strategy*)	ew or 1/N
Classical approach that ignores estimation error	
1. Sample-based mean-variance	mv
Bayesian approach to estimation error	
2. Bayesian diffuse-prior	Not reported
3. Bayes-Stein	bs
4. Bayesian Data-and-Model	dm
Moment restrictions	
5. Minimum-variance	min
6. Value-weighted market portfolio	vw
7. MacKinlay and Pastor's (2000) missing-factor model	mp
Portfolio constraints	
8. Sample-based mean-variance with short-sale constraints	mv-c
9. Bayes-Stein with short-sale constraints	bs-c
10. Minimum-variance with short-sale constraints	Min-c
11. Minimum-variance with generalized constraints	g-min-c
Optimal combinations of portfolios	
12. Kan and Zhou's (2007) "three-fund" model	mv-min
13. Mixture of minimum-variance and 1/N	ew-min
14. Garlappi, Uppal, and Wang's (2007) multi-prior model	Not reported

But the authors didn't stop there. They did the analysis of the different asset allocation techniques on *eight different datasets* to ensure their findings were robust. They examined a variety of sector portfolios, country portfolios, factor portfolios, and even generated simulated data for their horse race across the different asset allocation approaches (see Table 6.6).

What they found was remarkable. *Equal-weight portfolios meet or beat all of the fancy portfolios.* Table 6.7 summarizes the Sharpe ratio results from the original paper. You'll quickly note that the equal-weight strategy has robust performance across the various test assets relative to the fancier alternatives. You'll also identify that the in-sample mean-variance (labeled "mv (in-sample)") stats are amazing, but they are also unattainable in a real-world trading environment (i.e., there is a look-ahead bias because we don't know the weights until after the period ends). Meanwhile, the out-of-sample mean-variance results (labeled "mv"), which we would earn if we were to pursue this strategy in the real world, are atrocious!

TABLE 6.6 Datasets Considered

# Dataset and Source	Number of Asset Classes Tested	Time Period	Abbreviation
1. Ten sector portfolios of the S&P 500 and the US equity market portfolio	11	01/1981–12/2002	S&P Sectors
2. Ten industry portfolios and the US equity market portfolio	11	07/1963–11/2004	Industry
3. Eight country indexes and the World Index	9	01/1970–07/2001	International
4. SMB and HML portfolios and the US equity market portfolio	3	07/1963–11/2004	MKT/SMB/HML
5. Twenty size- and book-to-market portfolios and the US equity MKT	21	07/1963–11/2004	FF-1-factor
6. Twenty size- and book-to-market portfolios and the MKT, SMB, and HML portfolios	23	07/1963–11/2004	FF-3-factor
7. Twenty size- and book-to-market portfolios and the MKT, SMB, HML, and UMD portfolios	24	07/1963–11/2004	FF-4-factor
8. Simulated data	10,25,50	2000 years	—

The punch line of the DeMiguel et al. article is stunning—equal-weight portfolios meet or beat all of the fancy portfolios. In their own words:

> We evaluate the out-of-sample performance of the sample-based mean-variance model, and its extensions designed to reduce estimation error, relative to the naive 1/N portfolio. Of the 14 models we evaluate across seven empirical datasets, none is consistently better than the 1/N rule in terms of Sharpe ratio, certainty-equivalent return, or turnover, which indicates that, out of sample, the gain from optimal diversification is more than offset by estimation error.[9]

The DeMiguel, Garlappi, and Uppal paper perplexed the academic establishment and drove home one of the key takeaways of successful asset

TABLE 6.7 Asset Allocation Models Empirical Results—Sharpe Ratios

Strategy	S&P sectors N = 11	Industry portfolios N = 11	Inter'l portfolios N = 9	Mkt/ SMB/HML N = 3	FF 1-factor N = 21	FF 4-factor N = 24
1/N	0.1876	0.1353	0.1277	0.2240	0.1623	0.1753
mv (in-sample)	0.3848	0.2124	0.2090	0.2851	0.5098	0.5364
mv	0.0794	0.0679	(0.0332)	0.2186	0.0128	0.1841
bs	0.0811	0.0719	(0.0297)	0.2536	0.0138	0.1791
dm (sa = 1.0%)	0.1410	0.0581	0.0707	0.0016	0.0004	0.2355
min	0.0820	0.1554	0.1490	0.2493	0.2778	(0.02)
vw	0.1444	0.1138	0.1239	0.1138	0.1138	0.1138
mp	0.1863	0.0533	0.0984	(0.00)	0.1238	0.1230
mv-c	0.0892	0.0678	0.0848	0.1084	0.1977	0.2024
bs-c	0.1075	0.0819	0.0848	0.1514	0.1955	0.2062
min-c	0.0834	0.1425	0.1501	0.2493	0.1546	0.3580
g-min-c	0.1371	0.1451	0.1429	0.2467	0.1615	0.3028
mv-min	0.0683	0.0772	(0.0353)	0.2546	(0.01)	0.1757
ew-min	0.1208	0.1576	0.1407	0.2503	0.2608	(0.02)

allocation: *Complexity does not necessarily add value.*[10] Simply stated, it is hard, and perhaps impossible, to do much better than 1/N in an hypercompetitive world with so much volatility and uncertainty.

BUT WHICH ASSETS DO WE CHOOSE?

Research suggests that an equal-weight approach works. It also seems reasonable that we approach the world as the endowments do and envision three core buckets: equity, real assets, and bonds. We could include alternatives in our setup, but this asset class can get messy and is generally terrible when we assess the FACTS outlined in the previous chapter. Let's keep the conversation practical for the do-it-yourself financial advisor.

How should we think about equity, real assets, and bonds? We believe that Mebane Faber and Eric Richardson's Ivy 5 portfolio achieves our goal with minimal brain damage (Figure 6.2).[11] They envision the world with five core asset classes, all equal-weighted at 20 percent:

- *Equity (40%)*
  - SP500 = SP500 Total Return Index (US stocks)
  - EAFE = MSCI EAFE Total Return Index (international stocks)

FIGURE 6.2   The IVY 5 Concept

- *Real assets (40%)*
  - REIT = FTSE NAREIT All Equity REITS Total Return Index (real estate)
  - GSCI = Goldman Sachs Commodity Index (commodities)
- *Bonds (20%)*
  - LTR = Merrill Lynch 7–10 year Government Bond Index (bonds)

The summary effect of this portfolio is a 40 percent allocation to equity (20 percent domestic and 20 percent foreign), a 40 percent allocation to real assets (20 percent real estate and 20 percent commodities), and a 20 percent allocation to bonds. Although this portfolio construct might not be optimal, we'll follow the advice from David Swensen, arguably one of the greatest asset allocators of our time, and "stick to a simple diversified portfolio, keep our costs down, and rebalance periodically to keep your asset allocations in line with your long-term goals."

SUMMARY

Chapter 6 began with some evidence demonstrating the fragile nature of complex asset allocation models. In investing, it is simplicity, and not complexity, that we should strive for. We reviewed the concept of diversification, and the Yale endowment's asset class mix, which appears complex but can be simplified into basic constituent asset classes available via publicly traded instruments. Additionally, the asset allocation decision itself can also be simplified. A study comparing allocation approaches found that a "naïve" 1/N strategy outperformed a range of more complex approaches. It would seem that this simplified rule can serve us quite well as an overarching asset allocation strategy.

NOTES

1. V. DeMiguel, L. Garlappi, and R. Uppal, "Optimal Versus Naïve Diversification: How Inefficient is the 1/N Portfolio Strategy?" *Review of Financial Studies* 22, no. 5 (2009): 1915–1953.

2. Jeff Benjamin, "Cliff Asness Says Market Volatility Is Reason to Diversify," *Investment News* (October 16, 2014), http://www.investmentnews.com/article/20141016/FREE/141019939/cliff-asness-says-market-volatility-is-a-good-reason-to-diversify.

3. "Investment Return of 20.2% Brings Yale Endowment Value to $23.9 Billion," *Yale News* (September 24, 2014), http://news.yale.edu/2014/09/24/investment-return-202-brings-yale-endowment-value-239-billion.

4. E. F. Schumacher, *Small Is Beautiful: Economics as if People Mattered* (London: Blond & Briggs, Ltd., 1973).

5. David W. Swensen, *Unconventional Success: A Fundamental Approach to Personal Investment* (New York: Simon & Schuster, 2005).

6. William J. Bernstein, *The Intelligent Asset Allocator: How to Build Your Portfolio to Maximize Returns and Minimize Risk* (New York: McGraw-Hill, 2001).

7. For the Swensen portfolio, we combine the 15 percent inflation-protected bonds exposure with the 15 percent conventional bond exposure because data on Treasury-Inflation-Protected Securities (TIPS) is limited. We have also done the analysis over the period when TIPS are available and the results are quantitatively similar.

8. Victor DeMiguel, Lorenzo Garlappi, and Raman Uppal, "Optimal Versus Naïve Diversification: How Inefficient Is the 1/N Portfolio Strategy?" *Review of Financial Studies* 22, no. 5 (2009): 1915–1953.

9. Ibid., p. 1915.

10. Additionally, Victor DeMiguel, Yuliya Plyakha, Raman Uppal, and Grigory Vilkov have been working on finding methods to improve the 1/N strategy. Their recent paper, "Improving Portfolio Selection Using Option-Implied Volatility and Skewness," *Journal of Financial and Quantitative Analysis* 48, no. 6 (December 2013), suggests that it might be possible to beat the equal-weight construct, but the analytical and data capabilities required are high.

11. Mebane T. Faber and Eric W. Richardson, *The Ivy Portfolio: How to Invest Like the Top Endowments and Avoid Bear Markets* (Hoboken, NJ: John Wiley & Sons, 2009).

CHAPTER 7

A Simple Risk Management Model That Works

"We find that by and large, these models [risk-management, or market-timing models] have predicted poorly both in-sample (IS) and out-of-sample (OOS) for 30 years ..."
> —Goyal and Welch, Comprehensive Look at the Empirical
> Performance of Equity Premium Prediction

Warning: The following chapter is highly "quant." If you enjoy programming, engineering, mathematical formulas, or took your prom date to the planetarium, this chapter is for you. On the other hand, if you are a newbie to the DIY universe, never fear. We have split this chapter into two sections. The first section gives you the key takeaways. Newbies and quants alike will enjoy this section. The second section drills down into the academic research behind the key takeaways. Good reading, but certainly not required to get the basics. Let's press onward!

* * *

Asset allocation is all well and good, but many investors, ourselves included, strive to manage risk to the utmost. If you have a great asset allocation model that drops by 40 percent when the market drops by 60 percent, are you smiling saying: "Isn't that great? I am beating the market by 20 percent!" Of course not. The art of preventing significant drawdowns, better known as risk management, is a well-studied field in high finance.

Like asset allocation, there are numerous hypotheses and competing arguments as to what approach works.

We have examined hundreds of risk-management, or *market-timing*, platforms over the years. You name it, we've probably seen it.

There are five broad "buckets" of risk management techniques:

1. Fundamental indicators—assess macroeconomic factors
2. Technical indicators—assess past prices, stock metrics
3. Sentiment indicators—assess investor sentiment levels
4. Variance indicators—assess volatility levels
5. Comprehensive indicator—make a hybrid approach using the techniques above

What Did We Find?

The sad conclusion is that few of these ideas stand up to intense robustness tests except for the simplest technical rules (much like asset allocation—simpler is often better). Trust us, we'd love to tell you that we have identified a way to reliably predict the market using fancy algorithms derived from hundreds of academic research articles. We've replicated these papers in one form or another and subjected their insights to intense empirical scrutiny. We've also tried to integrate the signals suggested from the research into a trading model we could deploy in the real world.

Not surprisingly, the Ivory Tower is a lot different than the real world. Few of the ideas are reliable: They lack robustness and they are littered with data mining. A large swath of the financial services industry would love to have you believe in the magic of market timing. We're here to tell you that you should be highly skeptical. But we aren't the only ones with this uneventful finding. Amit Goyal and Ivo Welch, in their 2008 paper, "A Comprehensive Look at the Empirical Performance of Equity Premium Prediction," come to a conclusion similar to our own:

> *Our article comprehensively reexamines the performance of variables that have been suggested by the academic literature to be good predictors of the equity premium. We find that by and large, these models have predicted poorly both in-sample (IS) and out-of-sample (OOS) for 30 years now; these models seem unstable, as diagnosed by their out-of-sample predictions and other statistics; and these models would not have helped an investor with access only to available information to profitably time the market.[1]*

At the outset, we did mention that simple technical rules—the simplest trading rules out there—are, ironically, the most robust and show the most promise for protecting against significant drawdowns. Granted, these rules are not meant to "beat the market" but rather allow a do-it-yourself investor to manage declines in the market easily and at low cost.

A SIMPLE RISK MANAGEMENT MODEL THAT WORKS

Simple moving average (MA) rules and time series momentum (TMOM) rules can protect capital for buy-and-hold investors during drawdown events. When we run the horserace between MA and TMOM, there is no clear winner. However, the empirical evidence shows that combining simple moving average rules and time series momentum rules enhances risk-adjusted performance, on average, of a portfolio. We call this system "robust," since it performs without failure under a wide range of conditions, environments, and time periods. Of course, in the context of financial markets, there is no such thing as "the ability to perform without failure," but the robust system does diversify risk management across two trading rules and provides more protection against benchmark drawdowns than all other systems we have analyzed. Let's explore this risk management technique in detail.

Simple Moving Average Rules (MA)

The simple moving average rule (MA) is, well, simple. The rule is as follows: You are allowed to buy an asset once the current price exceeds the simple moving average over the past N months; otherwise, do not buy the asset and stay in alternative assets (T-bills or cash). The N-month moving average is the simple equally weighted average for the past N months' closing prices. This well-known measure can be measured more formally as follows:

$$MA_t(N) = \frac{x_t + x_{t-1} + \cdots + x_{t-N+1}}{N}$$

where
x_t = price at month t
N = number of periods in the moving average

An example shown in Table 7.1 outlines how the trading rule would work in practice. Consider a hypothetical market index price of 25.

In the example, the current price at $t = 12$ is 23.504, which is less than the 12-month moving average of 24.42. The MA trading rule would suggest that we stay in cash, as the current price (23.504) is below the current 12-month average (24.42).

TABLE 7.1 Example Simple Moving Average Calculation

Date	Price	Return
0	25	
1	24.263	−2.95%
2	24.141	−0.50%
3	24.214	0.30%
4	24.502	1.19%
5	24.384	−0.48%
6	24.716	1.36%
7	24.980	1.07%
8	24.850	−0.52%
9	24.905	0.22%
10	24.599	−1.23%
11	23.942	−2.67%
12	23.504	−1.83%
12-Month Simple Moving Average	24.42	

Time Series Momentum Rules (TMOM)

Time series momentum rule (TMOM) buys assets when excess return is greater than zero and invests into the alternative assets (e.g., cash or money market) when the excess return is less than zero. The excess return is measured as the total return over the past N months less the return of the Treasury bill (one could use other benchmarks). TMOM can be measured more formally as follows:

$$TMOM_t(N) = \left(\frac{x_t}{x_{t-N}} - 1 \right) - rf$$

where
x_t = price of month t
N = number of periods
rf = risk-free return or the return of the Treasury bill

The example in Table 7.2 outlines how the time series momentum trading rule (TMOM) would work in practice for a 12-month version of the rule ($N = 12$). Consider a hypothetical market index price of 25 and a Treasury-bill return of one percent over the past 12 months.

In the example, the past 12-month return is −5.99 percent and the Treasury bill return was 1 percent. Because the asset's return (−5.99%) is less than the Treasury-bill return (1%), the TMOM trading rule would suggest

TABLE 7.2 Example Time Series Momentum Calculation

Date	Price	Return
0	25	
1	24.263	−2.95%
2	24.141	−0.50%
3	24.214	0.30%
4	24.502	1.19%
5	24.384	−0.48%
6	24.716	1.36%
7	24.980	1.07%
8	24.850	−0.52%
9	24.905	0.22%
10	24.599	−1.23%
11	23.942	−2.67%
12	23.504	−1.83%
12-Month Cumulative Return		**−5.99%**

that we sit in cash until the return on the risky asset over the past 12 months exceeds the Treasury-bill return over the past 12 months.

Combining MA and MOM Is ROBUST

The examples above outline the moving average and the time series momentum trading rules. As it turns out, there is indeed a formal relationship between MA and TMOM trading rules. We examine the formal relationship between MA and TMOM using basic mathematics. If you are quantitatively challenged, feel free to skip the equations and move on to the figures that follow.

First some definitions:

- Define MA as follows: $MA_t(N) = \frac{x_t + x_{t-1} + \cdots + x_{t-N+1}}{N}$ (N period moving average calculated at time t).
- Define TMOM as follows: $TMOM_t(N) = \left(\frac{x_t}{x_{t-N}} - 1\right) - rf$ (N period excess return calculated at t).

Step 1: Take a difference between the MA at time t and the MA at time $t - 1$, and get the following formula:

$$MA_t(N) - MA_{t-1}(N) = \frac{x_t - x_{t-N}}{N} \tag{1}$$

Step 2: Then we break down the TMOM formula as follows:

$$TMOM_t(N) = \left(\frac{x_t}{x_{t-N}} - 1\right) - rf = \left(\frac{x_t - x_{t-N}}{x_{t-N}}\right) - rf$$

$$= \left(\frac{x_t - x_{t-N}}{N}\right)\frac{N}{x_{t-N}} - rf \qquad (2)$$

Step 3: We can get the following relationships between formulas (1) and (2):

$$TMOM_t(N) = (MA_t(N) - MA_{t-1}(N))\frac{N}{x_{t-N}} - rf$$

Step 3 highlights that TMOM and MA are mathematically related, but different. TMOM is a function of a current and a lagged MA rule. A majority of the time, the TMOM and MA rules will indicate the same action, however, the two rules, while similar, are not equal. To visually see how MA and TMOM can come to different conclusions, examine the sample price simulations in Figure 7.1 and Figure 7.2. Figure 7.1 highlights a scenario where MA rules are positive because there hasn't been a sharp downturn, but TMOM is negative because the past 12-month excess performance is negative.

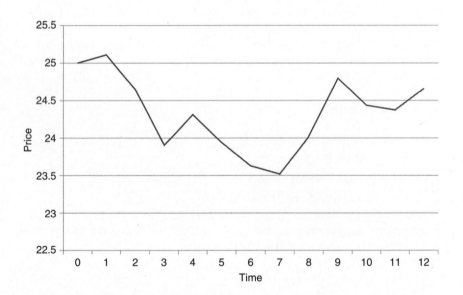

FIGURE 7.1 TMOM = Bad; MA = Good

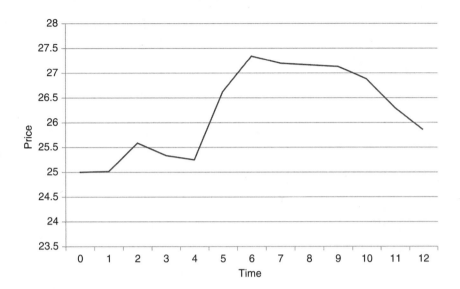

FIGURE 7.2 TMOM = Good; MA = Bad

Figure 7.2 also uses simulated price data and shows that there can be a scenario where the past 12 month excess performance is positive, but because of a sharp turn in recent performance, the MA rule is negative. Of course, in general, MA and TMOM point in the same direction, however, Figures 7.1 and 7.2 highlight that this conclusion is not inevitable.

As the equations highlight, TMOM and MA rules are tied together: Time series momentum rules (TMOM) are a function of moving average (MA) rules. And while TMOM and MA triggers are highly correlated, there are circumstances where the rules have a difference of opinion (see Figures 7.1 and 7.2). Our analysis suggests that this "difference of opinion," where one rule zigs while the other zags, creates a trading rule (ROBUST) that is more resilient than either trading rule as a stand-alone risk management device.

HOW DOES ROBUST WORK?

In this following section, we show performances for the simplest risk-management models that seem to work: MA, MOM, and ROBUST.[2] We look at how each of these systems performs on the five asset classes outlined below:

- SPX = S&P 500 Total Return Index (US Stocks)
- EAFE = MSCI EAFE Total Return Index (International Stocks)

- REIT = FTSE NAREIT All Equity REITS Total Return Index (Real Estate)
- GSCI = S&P GSCI Total Return CME (Commodities)
- LTR = The Merrill Lynch 10-year US Treasury Futures Total Return Index (Bonds)

The results presented are gross, and no fees are included. All returns are total returns and include the reinvestment of distributions (e.g., dividends). Proceeds are invested in treasury bills when a risk management rule is triggered.

Buy-and-hold results for the five asset classes from January 1976 to December 2014 are presented in Table 7.3.

Time Series Momentum (TMOM)

We apply a 12-month time series momentum (TMOM) strategy on the five asset classes from January 1976 to December 2014. The results are shown in Table 7.4.

Notice the reduction in downside deviation and worst drawdown. The results illustrate that time series momentum (TMOM) works better on a risk–adjusted basis than simply buying and holding the Ivy 5 asset classes on a standalone basis. Sharpe and Sortino ratios are uniformly better across the five asset classes.

Simple Moving Average (MA)

We repeat this exercise with a 12-month moving average (MA) strategy. The results are shown in Table 7.5 and are similar to Table 7.4: All generate higher Sharpe and Sortino ratios relative to a buy-and-hold strategy (shown in Table 7.3).

TABLE 7.3 Summary Statistics for IVY 5 (1/1976–12/2014)

Buy and Hold	SPX	EAFE	REIT	GSCI	LTR
CAGR	11.74%	9.44%	13.67%	5.64%	8.55%
Standard Deviation	15.01%	17.04%	16.92%	19.15%	8.37%
Downside Deviation	11.01%	12.09%	14.48%	13.56%	5.21%
Sharpe Ratio	0.50	0.33	0.56	0.13	0.45
Sortino Ratio (MAR = 5%)	0.66	0.46	0.65	0.17	0.69
Worst Drawdown	−50.21%	−56.68%	−68.30%	−69.38%	−20.97%
Worst Month Return	−21.58%	−20.18%	−31.67%	−28.20%	−8.41%
Best Month Return	13.52%	15.58%	31.02%	22.94%	15.23%
Profitable Months	62.61%	59.53%	63.60%	56.75%	64.03%

TABLE 7.4 Time Series Momentum (TMOM) Performance (1/1976–12/2014)

TMOM RULE	SPX	EAFE	REIT	GSCI	LTR
CAGR	11.78%	9.69%	14.43%	8.63%	9.17%
Standard Deviation	11.90%	11.86%	12.19%	15.23%	5.94%
Downside Deviation	9.47%	9.14%	9.37%	12.57%	4.15%
Sharpe Ratio	0.59	0.44	0.78	0.31	0.70
Sortino Ratio (MAR = 5%)	0.73	0.55	0.99	0.36	0.96
Worst Drawdown	−29.58%	−25.72%	−19.98%	−55.02%	−6.41%
Worst Month Return	−21.58%	−14.01%	−15.24%	−28.20%	−5.71%
Best Month Return	13.52%	14.06%	14.28%	22.94%	8.73%
Profitable Months	73.93%	75.64%	74.57%	77.56%	78.63%

TABLE 7.5 Moving Average (MA) Performance (1/1976–12/2014)

MA RULE	SPX	EAFE	REIT	GSCI	LTR
CAGR	11.56%	10.62%	13.85%	7.88%	8.43%
Standard Deviation	12.00%	12.45%	12.17%	15.19%	7.11%
Downside Deviation	9.38%	9.35%	9.29%	11.35%	4.85%
Sharpe Ratio	0.57	0.49	0.74	0.26	0.50
Sortino Ratio (MAR = 5%)	0.72	0.63	0.95	0.33	0.70
Worst Drawdown	−23.58%	−21.07%	−20.78%	−52.38%	−11.26%
Worst Month Return	−21.58%	−14.01%	−15.24%	−14.41%	−8.41%
Best Month Return	13.52%	14.06%	12.60%	22.94%	14.10%
Profitable Months	72.01%	72.65%	72.22%	72.65%	71.79%

TMOM and MA Horse Race

OK. So it looks like TMOM and MA have some empirical horsepower ... but which is better? We compare the performance between TMOM and MA in Table 7.6. Table 7.6 shows that both strategies generate favorable Sharpe and Sortino ratios across the asset classes. To identify a "winner" between TMOM and MA, we consider it a win if the Sharpe and Sortino are higher; we consider it a loss if the Sharpe and Sortino are lower; and we consider it a tie if the Sharpe and Sortino come to mixed conclusions (e.g., Sharpe is higher but Sortino is lower). Based on this analysis, TMOM wins on all the asset classes, save EAFE, giving the TMOM system an edge in the horse race between TMOM and MA. However, despite a small edge for TMOM, the reality is that the risk-adjusted metrics are similar across the board for both TMOM and MA, and both systems add value as a risk-management tool.

TABLE 7.6   MOM VS. MA Performance Comparisons (1/1976–12/2014)

	Sharpe	Sortino	Winner
SPX_MA	.57	.72	
SPX_TMOM	.59	.73	X
EAFE_MA	.49	.63	X
EAFE_TMOM	.44	.55	
REIT_MA	.74	.95	
REIT_TMOM	.78	.99	X
GSCI_MA	.26	.33	
GSCI_TMOM	.31	.36	X
LTR_MA	.50	.70	
LTR_TMOM	.70	.96	X

Combining TMOM and MA (ROBUST)

There are more complex methods to combine two strategies, but here we just apply a simple combination rule that is 50 percent invested in the TMOM strategy and 50 percent invested in the MA strategy. We label the 50/50 system, ROBUST. ROBUST invests in T-bills when a trading rule triggers. Because of the 50/50 nature, ROBUST can either be 100 percent allocated (both TMOM and MA flash green), 50 percent allocated (either TMOM or MA flash green, but not both), or 0 percent allocated (both TMOM and MA flash red) to a given asset class at a given point in time. Table 7.7 illustrates the performance of ROBUST.

ROBUST performance is strong across the five asset classes. Table 7.8 conducts the head-to-head analysis between TMOM, MA, and ROBUST.

TABLE 7.7   ROBUST Performance (1/1976–12/2014)

MA RULE	SPX	EAFE	REIT	GSCI	LTR
CAGR	11.71%	10.21%	14.18%	8.34%	8.82%
Standard Deviation	11.61%	11.71%	11.85%	14.74%	6.22%
Downside Deviation	9.20%	8.72%	9.08%	11.25%	4.07%
Sharpe Ratio	0.60	0.48	0.78	0.29	0.62
Sortino Ratio (MAR = 5%)	0.74	0.62	1.00	0.37	0.90
Worst Drawdown	−26.30%	−19.28%	−18.30%	−51.47%	−6.41%
Worst Month Return	−21.58%	−14.01%	−15.24%	−14.41%	−5.71%
Best Month Return	13.52%	14.06%	12.60%	22.94%	8.73%
Profitable Months	72.01%	71.58%	72.44%	72.01%	72.65%

TABLE 7.8 ROBUST Performance Comparisons (1/1976–12/2014)

	Sharpe	Sortino	Winner
SPX_MA	.57	.72	
SPX_TMOM	.59	.73	
SPX_ROBUST	.60	.74	X
EAFE_MA	.49	.63	
EAFE_TMOM	.44	.55	
EAFE_ROBUST	.48	.62	Tie
REIT_MA	.74	.95	
REIT_TMOM	.78	.99	
REIT_ROBUST	.78	1.00	X
GSCI_MA	.26	.33	
GSCI_TMOM	.31	.36	
GSCI_ROBUST	.29	.37	Tie
LTR_MA	.50	.70	
LTR_TMOM	.70	.96	X
LTR_ROBUST	.62	.90	

While there is certainly an element of "splitting hairs" across the models (they are all a lot better than buy and hold), the evidence suggests that combining the two technical rules seems to be the strongest performer.[3]

Out-of-Sample Tests

The previous analysis is interesting because it applies to the five large asset classes that all investors know and love. To explore the benefits of MA, TMOM, and ROBUST, we look elsewhere for additional data. Specifically, we examine the following data sets:

- SPX = S&P 500 Total Return Index (January 1928 to December 1975, which is prior to time period previously examined)
- NKY = Nikkei 225 Index (January 1971 to December 2014—Japanese Stocks)
- DAX = Deutsche Boerse AG German Stock Index (October 1960 to December 2014)

The empirical results presented are gross, and no fees are included. The S&P 500 returns are total returns and include the reinvestment of distributions (e.g., dividends), but for the NKY and DAX we only use the price-based indices (the total return indices have much shorter histories, so we rely on the price-only indices for this analysis).

TABLE 7.9   SPX Performance Across Systems (1/1928 to 12/1975)

	SPX B&H	SPX ROBUST	SPX TMOM	SPX MA
CAGR	8.04%	8.57%	8.23%	8.78%
Standard Deviation	21.94%	12.61%	13.01%	13.13%
Downside Deviation	16.14%	10.14%	10.46%	10.66%
Sharpe Ratio	0.36	0.54	0.50	0.54
Sortino Ratio (MAR = 5%)	0.32	0.40	0.36	0.41
Worst Drawdown	−84.59%	−49.95%	−53.42%	−48.65%
Worst Month Return	−28.73%	−23.13%	−23.13%	−23.13%
Best Month Return	41.65%	17.56%	17.56%	17.56%
Profitable Months	60.76%	73.44%	76.04%	75.35%

SPX – US Stocks   ROBUST, TMOM, and MA work well for SPX data from January 1928 to December 1975, ROBUST and MA are virtually tied: Their Sharpe ratios are equivalent and the MA Sortino ratio is .43 versus .42 (see Table 7.9).

NKY – Japanese Stocks   Investing in the Japanese stock market has been tough for the buy-and-hold investor—offering a 5.06 percent compounded annual return coupled with a greater than 80 percent drawdown. It is important to note that if we had data on the total return performance, which is unavailable, it would look slightly better. Of course, the risk-managed versions of the price-only NKY index are not much better, with compound annual returns in the 6 percent range and drawdowns between 40 and 50 percent. Nonetheless, the risk-managed versions worked better than buy and hold. The best system was TMOM, with ROBUST coming in as a close second, and with a slightly lower maximum drawdown (see Table 7.10).

TABLE 7.10   NKY Performance Across Systems (1/1971 to 12/2014)

	NKY B&H	NKY ROBUST	NKY TMOM	NKY MA
CAGR	5.06%	6.61%	6.90%	6.18%
Standard Deviation	19.15%	12.26%	12.90%	12.72%
Downside Deviation	13.77%	8.80%	9.12%	9.14%
Sharpe Ratio	0.10	0.18	0.20	0.15
Sortino Ratio (MAR = 5%)	0.13	0.25	0.28	0.20
Worst Drawdown	−80.55%	−42.98%	−43.27%	−45.29%
Worst Month Return	−23.83%	−16.73%	−16.73%	−16.73%
Best Month Return	20.07%	16.27%	16.27%	16.27%
Profitable Months	55.68%	71.40%	74.24%	73.86%

TABLE 7.11 DAX Performance Across Systems (1/1961 to 12/2014)

	DAX B&H	DAX ROBUST	DAX TMOM	DAX MA
CAGR	5.54%	6.16%	6.28%	5.91%
Standard Deviation	19.27%	13.51%	14.02%	13.84%
Downside Deviation	13.52%	9.67%	9.97%	9.65%
Sharpe Ratio	0.13	0.16	0.17	0.14
Sortino Ratio (MAR = 5%)	0.17	0.20	0.21	0.18
Worst Drawdown	−68.28%	−32.45%	−35.63%	−37.95%
Worst Month Return	−25.42%	−21.52%	−21.52%	−21.52%
Best Month Return	21.38%	18.01%	18.01%	18.01%
Profitable Months	56.48%	71.30%	74.54%	73.92%

DAX – German Stocks The German stock market has also had a tough run relative to the S&P 500, but it has performed better than the Japanese market. Based on risk-adjusted statistics, it is hard to ascertain a strong benefit to the ROBUST, MOM, or MA timing systems. TMOM has the strongest showing across Sharpe and Sortino ratios, but the Sharpe and Sortino ratios for a buy-and-hold strategy are not far behind. However, the risk-management systems shine when it comes to drawdown protection. The timing models cut the drawdown in half. ROBUST is the most favorable and takes the drawdown from over 68 percent to just over 32 percent—still painful, but not life-threatening (see Table 7.11).

Additional Tests We have done extensive analysis on technical trading rules. In general, simple technical rules work just as well, or better, than complex technical rules. Also, technical rules, such as the moving average rule, don't beat buy and hold all the time. For example, if one starts an S&P 500 dataset in 1938 and runs it through 2013, the simple moving average rule is arguably no better than buy and hold. This is a cherry-picked start date, but the point is that there is no silver bullet and risk is inevitable, regardless of how you manage it. One must always consider the very real possibility of downside potential.

Why Might Technical Rules Work? So the results behind these rules appear robust; however, the greater question is, *why* do they work? One would think that everyone in the market would simply deploy these risk management tools, thereby rendering them ineffective, right?

We believe there is a behavioral story underlying the success of simple technical trading rules. Consider the concept of dynamic risk aversion, which is the idea that human beings don't view risk and reward the same way all of the time—our appetite for risk changes, depending on our recent experiences. For example, imagine we are making a decision to build a new house in California along the San Andreas Fault. If we had just lived through an earthquake, taking on the risk of building a new house on the San Andreas Fault is probably scary, even though the probability of another earthquake hasn't changed. In contrast, when there hasn't been an earthquake in 50 years, building a new house along a fault is not a big deal. In this case, we may perceive the likelihood of an earthquake as being lower than it really is. As this example shows, our perception of risk is not constant and can change based on recent experience. But how does our ever-changing perception of risk matter in the context of financial markets?

Economists often assume that risk aversion, or our willingness to accept risk, is independent of our recent experience. In other words, how we feel about risk will be independent of whether or not we lived through an earthquake 5 minutes ago or 50 years ago. Another assumption economists sometimes make is that risk, often measured in terms of standard deviation, or *volatility*, is relatively constant. These assumptions create a puzzle in the context of extreme stock market drawdowns where the prices of stocks seem to go down further than fundamentals would suggest they should.

What is so puzzling about a 50 percent market drawdown, when, say, the fundamentals suggest the market should only take a 20 percent haircut? Well, as prices move down 20 percent, economists assume that because expected returns have gone up after prices have moved down, and volatility and risk aversion are assumed to be relatively constant, investors should swoop in to buy up cheap shares to ensure they don't drop below 20 percent, which in our example is their so-called fundamental value. But that doesn't happen. If it did, Warren Buffett would be unemployed and markets much calmer than they are. However, stocks can—and have—gone down over 50 percent, and these movements are much more volatile than the underlying dividends and cash flows of the stocks they represent!

How is this possible in a rational market? One approach to understanding this puzzle is by relaxing the assumption that investors maintain a constant aversion to risk. Consider the possibility that investors dynamically change their view on risk after a steep 20 percent drawdown (i.e., they just lived through an earthquake); even though expected returns go up dramatically, risk aversion also shoots up dramatically, which means prices have to go down a lot further to justify an investor to buy these "cheap" stocks. This increased aversion to risk, following a steep price drop, leads to more selling, and more selling leads to even more hatred for risk, which leads to more selling, and so forth. What you end up is a stampede for the exits and an intense selloff in the marketplace—well beyond what a traditional economist would consider "rational."

This discussion is a simplified story of investor psychology in the context of a stock-market drawdown. For exposition purposes, we are leaving out many potentially important details. However, details aside, if one believes that investors recalibrate their tolerance for risk during a market debacle, and tend to sell shares at any price, this might help explain why long-term trend-following rules, which systematically get an investor out of a cliff-diving bear market before everyone has jumped ship, have worked over time. Of course, technical rules will only work if the massive bear doesn't happen in a short time period before the long-term trend rules can signal an exit. Technical rules will not save an investor from a 1987 type "flash" crash, but they can save an investor from a 1929 or a 2008 type crash, which can take a few months to develop. And as long as the bull rally following an epic bear market doesn't come fast and furious, long-term trend rules will allow the investor to participate in a substantial portion of the upside. In the end, if one believes in a price dynamic that involves steep and relatively sharp declines, followed by slow grinding uphill climbs, simple technical rules will, by design, improve risk-adjusted performance.

SUMMARY

Simple technical rules, in the form of simple moving averages (MA) or time series momentum (TMOM), seem to be useful in a risk-management context. Will they continue to work in the future? Who knows, but market psychology seems to suggest they'll continue to be useful. These trading rules lower drawdown risk but allow the investor to participate in a lot of the upside associated with a given asset class. Trying to determine the "best" technical rule is somewhat arbitrary—both MA and TMOM are useful. Our analysis suggests that there is no reason to limit ourselves to one of the technical rules. We can do a simple 50/50 split between the rules and generate an excellent risk-reward profile with the ROBUST system. The beauty of the ROBUST framework is that a do-it-yourself investor can understand, implement, and be successful with the strategy.

RISK MANAGEMENT RESEARCH (FOR GEEKS ONLY)

Fundamental Indicators

We consider a variety of research articles that examine timing indicators related to the macroeconomic environment. This line of research typically involves data from the bureau of labor statistics or data related to assets in the marketplace, which are thought to drive economic success or failure (e.g., oil prices). Here we describe some interesting ideas in this line of research.

Consumption, Aggregate Wealth, and Expected Stock Returns

- Lettau and Ludvigson (2002): "*This paper studies the role of fluctuations in the aggregate consumption–wealth ratio for predicting stock returns. Using U.S. quarterly stock market data, we find that these fluctuations in the consumption–wealth ratio are strong predictors of both real stock returns and excess returns over a Treasury bill rate.*"[4]

Adaptive Macro Indexes and Short-term Variation in Stock Returns

- Bai (2010) Adaptive Macro Indexes: "*Fundamental economic conditions are crucial determinants of equity premia … I find that adaptive macro indexes explain a substantial fraction of the short-term variation in future stock returns and have more forecasting power than both the historical average of stock returns and commonly used predictors.*"[5]

Industrial Metal Returns

- Jacobsen, Marshall, and Visaltanachoti (2013): "*Price movements in industrial metals, such as copper and aluminum, predict stock returns worldwide. Increasing metal prices are good news for equity markets in recessions and bad news in expansions. Industrial metals returns forecast changes in the economy and information gradually diffuses from metals to stocks through both the discount rate and cash flow channels. Out-of-sample R2's are as high as 9%.*"[6]

Oil Shocks and Market Returns

- Kilian and Park (2007): "*It is shown that the reaction of U.S. real stock returns to an oil price shock differs greatly depending on whether the change in the price of oil is driven by demand or supply shocks in the oil market. The demand and supply shocks driving the global crude oil market jointly account for 22% of the long-run variation in U.S. real stock returns.*"[7]

Market-Wide Earning-Return Relation

- Sadka (2009): "*This paper studies the effects of predictability on the earnings–returns relation for individual firms and for the aggregate. We demonstrate that prices better anticipate earnings growth at the aggregate level than at the firm level, which implies that random-walk models are inappropriate for gauging aggregate earnings expectations.*"[8]

Cyclically Adjusted PE Ratio (CAPE)

■ Campbell and Shiller (1998): *"The price-smoothed earnings ratio ... is a good forecaster of ten-year growth in stock prices, with an R^2 statistics of 37%."*

■ Siegel (2013): *"The CAPE ratio was calculated by taking a broad-based index of stock market prices, such as the S&P 500, and dividing by the average of the last ten years of aggregate earnings, all measured in real terms. The CAPE ratio was then regressed against the future ten-year real returns on stocks, establishing that the CAPE ratio was a significant variable predicting long-run stock returns.*[9]

Implied Cost of Capital (ICC)

■ Li, Ng, and Swaminathan (2013): *"Theoretically, the implied cost of capital (ICC) is a good proxy for time-varying expected returns. We find that aggregate ICC strongly predicts future excess market returns at horizons ranging from one month to four years ... We also find that ICC s of size and B/M portfolios predict corresponding portfolio returns."*[10]

Sum of the Parts Forecasting

■ Ferreira and Santa-Clara (2011): *"We propose forecasting separately the three components of stock market returns—the dividend–price ratio, earnings growth, and price–earnings ratio growth—the sum-of-the-parts (SOP) method. Our method exploits the different time-series persistence of the components and obtains out-of-sample R-squares (compared with the historical mean) of more than 1.3% with monthly data and 13.4% with yearly data."*[11]

Technical Indicators

Technical indicators have been written off as heresy by many academics. The biggest complaint is that technical trading rules rely on past prices to predict futures returns. This concept flies in the face of the efficient market hypothesis, and therefore requires researchers to jump over a high bar to get their research published in a peer-reviewed journal. As academics, we understand this skepticism with technical trading rules, but as empiricists, we are willing to give any idea a fair shot. Below are some of the more interesting research papers on the subject.

Time Series Momentum

■ Moskowitz, Ooi, and Pedersen (2010): *"We document significant 'time series momentum' in equity index, currency, commodity, and*

bond futures for each of the 58 liquid instruments we consider...
A diversified portfolio of time series momentum strategies across all
asset classes delivers substantial abnormal returns with little exposure
to standard asset pricing factors and performs best during extreme
markets."[13]

Time-Varying Sharpe Ratios

- Tang and Whitelaw (2011): *"This paper documents predictable*
  time-variation in stock market Sharpe ratios. ... In sample, estimated
  conditional Sharpe ratios show substantial time-variation that coincides
  with the phases of the business cycle. Generally, Sharpe ratios are low at
  the peak of the cycle and high at the trough. In an out-of-sample anal-
  ysis, using 10-year rolling regressions, relatively naive market-timing
  strategies that exploit this predictability can identify periods with
  Sharpe ratios more than 45% larger than the full sample value."[14]

Simple Moving Average (MA) Rules

- Faber (2007): *"This article presents a simple quantitative method*
  that improves risk-adjusted returns across various asset classes.
  A moving-average timing model is tested in-sample on the United
  States equity market and out-of-sample on more than twenty additional
  domestic and foreign markets."[15]

Challenging MA Rule #1

- Scholz and Walther (2011): *"The often reported empirical success of*
  trend-following technical timing strategies remains to be puzzling...
  We claim that empirical timing success is possible even in perfectly
  efficient markets but does not indicate prediction power. We prove this
  by systematically tracing back timing success to the statistical charac-
  teristics of the underlying asset price time series, which is modeled by
  standard stochastic processes."[16]

Challenging MA Rule #2

- Zakamulin (2014): *"These active timing strategies (including Faber's*
  MA rule) are very appealing to investors because of their extraordinary
  simplicity and because they promise substantial advantages over their
  passive counterparts. However, the 'too good to be true' reported per-
  formance of these market timing rules raises a legitimate concern as to
  whether this performance is realistic and whether investors can expect
  that future performance will be the same as the documented historical
  performance. We argue that the reported performance of market timing

strategies usually contains a considerable data-mining bias and ignores important market frictions."[17]

Challenging MA Rule #3

- Marmi, Pacati, Risso, Reno (2012): "*...*"*A quantitative approach to tactical asset allocation*" *by the fund manager M. Faber, a real hit in the SSRN online library. Is this paper a counterexample to market efficiency? We reject this conclusion, showing that a lot of caution should be used in this field, and we indicate a series of bootstrapping experiments which can be easily implemented to evaluate the performance of trading strategies.*"[18]

Overview of Technical Analysis

- Park and Irwin (2007): "*The purpose of this report is to review the evidence on the profitability of technical analysis. To achieve this purpose, the report comprehensively reviews survey, theoretical and empirical studies regarding technical trading strategies.*"[19]

Dual Momentum Investing

- Antonacci (2014): "*By combining relative-strength momentum and absolute momentum, this unique methodology lets you take advantage of intra-market trends while avoiding large drawdowns.*"[20]

Sentiment Indicators

Malcolm Baker and Jeff Wurgler in their 2006 paper "Investor Sentiment and the Cross-section of Stock Returns" make a clear statement: "Classical finance theory leaves no role for investor sentiment."[21] They go on to highlight that investor sentiment might play a significant role in explaining return differences among stocks. If sentiment appears to work in stock selection, one might reasonably suppose that sentiment plays a role in market timing. One idea might be that high investor sentiment represents euphoria, which predicts low future returns, and low investor sentiment represents excess pessimism, which predicts high future returns. These ideas have been explored in the academic literature and we highlight a few papers below.

Investor Sentiment Indicators

- Baker, Wurgler, and Yuan (2010): "*We construct investor sentiment indices for six major stock markets and decompose them into one global and six local indices ... Global sentiment is a contrarian predictor of country-level returns. Both global and local sentiment are contrarian predictors of the time series of cross-sectional returns within markets: When sentiment is high, future returns are low on relatively difficult to arbitrage and difficult to value stocks."*[22]

- Zouaoui, Nouyrigat, and Beer (2011): *"We test the impact of investor sentiment on a panel of international stock markets. Specifically, we examine the influence of investor sentiment on the probability of stock market crises. We find that investor sentiment increases the probability of occurrence of stock market crises within a one-year horizon. The impact of investor sentiment on stock markets is more pronounced in countries that are culturally more prone to herd-like behavior, overreaction and low institutional involvement."*[23]

- Huang, Tu, Jiang, and Zhou (2014): *"We propose a new investor sentiment index that is aligned with the purpose of predicting the aggregate stock market. By eliminating a common noise component in sentiment proxies, the new index has much greater predictive power than existing sentiment indices both in- and out-of-sample, and the predictability becomes both statistically and economically significant."*[24]

The Equity Share in New Issues and Aggregate Stock Returns

- Baker and Wurgler (2000): *"The share of equity issues in total new equity and debt issues is a strong predictor of U.S. stock market returns between 1928 and 1997. In particular, firms issue relatively more equity than debt just before periods of low market returns. The equity share in new issues has stable predictive power in both halves of the sample period and after controlling for other known predictors."*[25]

Aggregate Net Exchanges of Equity Funds/Mutual Fund Flows

- Ben-Rephael, Kandel, and Wohl (2011): *"We investigate a proxy for monthly shifts between bond funds and equity funds in the USA: aggregate net exchanges of equity funds. This measure (which is negatively related to changes in VIX) is positively contemporaneously correlated with aggregate stock market excess returns: One standard deviation of net exchanges is related to 1.95% of market excess return. These findings support the notion of "noise" in aggregate market prices induced by investor sentiment."*[26]

Are Discounts on Closed-End Funds a Sentiment Index?

- Chen, Kan, and Miller (1993): *"In sum, we reject as unfounded the central claim of Lee et al. that 'The evidence suggests that discounts on closed-end funds are indeed a proxy for changes in individual investor sentiment and that same sentiment affects returns of smaller capitalization stocks and other stocks held and traded by individual investors.'"*[27]

Yes, Discounts on Closed-End Funds Are a Sentiment Index

- Chopra, Lee, Shleifer, Thaler (1993): "*In summary, none of the stones Chen, Kan and Miller (CKM) throw seem to have hit. There is nothing embarrassing for Lee et al. in the fact that utility stocks rise when fund discounts narrow.*"[28]

Short Interest and Aggregate Market Returns

- Rapach, Ringgenberg, and Zhou (2014): "*We show that aggregate short interest is one of the strongest known predictors of the equity risk premium. High aggregate short interest predicts lower future equity returns at monthly, quarterly, semi-annual, and annual horizons.*"[29]

Volatility-Based Indicators

Risk and return are linked in financial markets. If you take on more risk, you generally can expect to earn a higher return, and vice versa. *Risk* is often measured in terms or standard deviation, which is deemed "volatility." And while more expected volatility usually means higher returns in the context of investing, researchers have asked a related question: Can we use market volatility to predict future market returns? The following papers explore a few ways in which researchers have tried to use volatility metrics to "predict the market."

Expected Stock Returns and Volatility

- French, Schwert, and Stambaugh (1987): "*This paper examines the relation between stock returns and stock market volatility. We find evidence that the expected market risk premium (the expected return on a stock portfolio minus the Treasury bill yield) is positively related to the predictable volatility of stock returns.*"[30]

Implied Volatility Spread

- Atilgan, Bali, and Demirtas (2014): "*This paper investigates the intertemporal relation between volatility spreads and expected returns on the aggregate stock market. We provide evidence for a significantly negative link between volatility spreads and expected returns at the daily and weekly frequencies. We argue that this link is driven by the information flow from option markets to stock markets.*"[31]
- Bali and Hovakimian (2009): "*We examine the relation between expected future volatility (options' implied volatility) and the cross-section of expected returns. A trading strategy buying stocks in the highest implied volatility quintile and shorting stocks in the lowest implied volatility quintile generates insignificant returns.*"[32]

Variance Risk Premia

- Bollerslev, Tauchen, and Zhou (2009): " ... *the difference between implied and realized variation, or the variance risk premium, is able to explain a nontrivial fraction of the time-series variation in post-1990 aggregate stock market returns, with high (low) premia predicting high (low) future returns.*"[33]

Market Volatility Index (VIX)

- Copeland and Copeland (1999): "*Changes in the Market Volatility Index (VIX) of the Chicago Board Options Exchange are statistically significant leading indicator of daily market returns. On days that follow increases in the VIX, portfolios of large-capitalization stocks outperform portfolios of small-capitalization stocks and value-based portfolios outperform growth-based portfolios. On days following a decrease in the VIX, the opposite occur.*"[34]

Tail Risk and Asset Prices

- Kelly and Jiang (2014): "*We propose a new measure of time-varying tail risk that is directly estimable from the cross-section of returns. We exploit firm-level price crashes every month to identify common fluctuations in tail risk among individual stocks. Our tail measure is significantly correlated with tail risk measures extracted from S&P 500 index options and negatively predicts real economic activity. We show that tail risk has strong predictive power for aggregate market returns.*"[35]

Comprehensive Summary of Different Predictors

Because there is such a glut of research trying to predict the stock market, some researchers have tried to combine various methodologies in an attempt to identify if there is a way to predict the market with a combination of factors.

- Neely, Rapach, Tu, and Zhou (2014): "*Our paper fills this gap by comparing the forecasting ability of technical indicators with that of macroeconomic variables. Technical indicators display statistically and economically significant in-sample and out-of-sample forecasting power, matching or exceeding that of macroeconomic variables ... we show that combining information from both technical indicators and macroeconomic variables significantly improves equity risk premium forecasts versus using either type of information alone.*"[36]
- Rapach and Zhou (2013): "*We survey the literature on stock return forecasting, highlighting the challenges faced by forecasters as well*

as strategies for improving return forecasts. We focus on U.S. equity premium forecastability and illustrate key issues via an empirical application based on updated data. Some studies argue that, despite extensive in-sample evidence of equity premium predictability, popular predictors from the literature fail to outperform the simple historical average benchmark forecast in out-of-sample tests. Recent studies, however, provide improved forecasting strategies that deliver statistically and economically significant out-of-sample gains relative to the historical average benchmark. These strategies—including economically motivated model restrictions, forecast combination, diffusion indices, and regime shifts—improve forecasting performance by addressing the substantial model uncertainty and parameter instability surrounding the data-generating process for stock returns. In addition to the U.S. equity premium, we succinctly survey out-of-sample evidence supporting U.S. cross-sectional and international stock return forecastability. The significant evidence of stock return forecastability worldwide has important implications for the development of both asset pricing models and investment management strategies."[37]

NOTES

1. Ivo Welch and Amit Goyal, "A Comprehensive Look at The Empirical Performance of Equity Premium Prediction," *Review of Financial Studies* 21, no. 4 (2008): 1455–1508.
2. If not specifically disclosed, we invest in Treasury bills when a trading rule triggered.
3. We perform sub-period analysis from February 1976 to December 1989 and January 1990 to July 2014 and come to similar conclusions.
4. Martin Lettau and Sydney Ludvigson, "Consumption, Aggregate Wealth, and Expected Stock Returns," *Journal of Finance* 56, no. 3 (2001): 815–849.
5. Jennie Bai, "Equity Premium Predictions with Adaptive Macro Indexes," Federal Reserve Bank of New York Staff Reports, no. 475 (2010).
6. Ben Jacobsen, Ben R. Marshall, and Nuttawat Visaltanachoti, "Stock Market Predictability and Industrial Metal Returns," 23rd Australasian Finance and Banking Conference 2010 Paper.
7. Lutz Kilian and Cheolbeom Park, "The Impact of Oil Price Shocks on the US Stock Market," *International Economic Review*, 50, no. 4 (2007): 1267–1287.
8. Gil Sadka and Ronnie Sadka, "Predictability and the Earnings–Returns Relation," *Journal of Financial Economics* 94, no. 1 (2009): 87–106.
9. John Y. Campbell and Robert J. Shiller, "Valuation Ratios and the Long-Run Stock Market Outlook," *Journal of Portfolio Management* 24, no. 2 (1998): 11–26.

10. Yan Li, David T. Ng, and Bhaskaran Swaminathan, "Predicting Market Returns Using Aggregate Implied Cost of Capital," *Journal of Financial Economics* (2013).

11. Miguel A. Ferreira and Pedro Santa-Clara, "Forecasting Stock Market Returns: The Sum of the Parts Is More than the Whole," *Journal of Financial Economics* 100 (2011): 87–106.

12. Lutz Kilian and Cheolbeom Park, "The Impact of Oil Price Shocks on the US Stock Market," *Journal of Financial Economics* 104 (2007): 228–250.

13. Toby Moskowitz, Yao Hua Ooi, and Lasse Pedersen, "Time Series Momentum," *Journal of Financial Economics* 104 (2012): 228–250.

14. Yi Tang and Robert F. Whitelaw, "Time-Varying Sharpe Ratios and Market Timing," *Journal of Finance* 1, no. 3 (2011): 465–493.

15. Mebane Faber Mebane, "A Quantitative Approach to Tactical Asset Allocation," *Journal of Wealth Management* 9, no. 4 (2006): 69–79.

16. Scholz Peter and Walther Ursula, "The Trend Is Not Your Friend! Why Empirical Timing Success Is Determined by the Underlying's Price Characteristics and Market Efficiency Is Irrelevant," CPQF Working Paper No. 29 (2011).

17. Valeriy Zakamulin, "The Real-Life Performance of Market Timing with Moving Average and Time-Series Momentum Rules," *Journal of Asset Management* 15 (2014): 261–278.

18. Stefano Marmi, Claudio Pacati, Wiston Adrian Risso, and Roberto Reno, "A Quantitative Approach to Faber's Tactical Asset Allocation," Working paper series (2012).

19. Cheol-Ho Park and Scott H. Irwin, "What Do We Know about the Profitability of Technical Analysis," *Journal of Economic Surveys* 21, no. 4 (2007): 786–826.

20. Gary Antonacci, *Dual-Momentum Investing*, 1st ed. (New York: McGraw-Hill, 2014).

21. Malcolm P. Baker and Jeffrey Wurgler, "Investor Sentiment and the Cross-Section of Stock Returns," *Journal of Finance* 61 (2006): 1645–1680.

22. Malcolm P. Baker, Jeffrey Wurgler, and Yu Yuan, "Global, Local, and Contagious Investor Sentiment," *Journal of Financial Economics* 104 (2010): 272–287.

23. Mohamed Zouaoui, Geneviève Nouyrigat, and Francisca Beer, "How Does Investor Sentiment Affect Stock Market Crises? Evidence from Panel Data," *Financial Review* 46, no. 4 (2011): 723–747.

24. Dashan Huang, Fuwei Jiang, Jun Tu, and Guofu Zhou, "Investor Sentiment Aligned: A Powerful Predictor of Stock Returns," *Review of Financial Studies* (2014).

25. Malcolm Baker and Jeffery Wurgler, "The Equity Share in New Issues and Aggregate Stock Returns," *Journal of Finance* 55, no. 5 (2000): 2219–2257.

26. Azi Ben-Rephael, Shmuel Kandel, and Avi Wohl, "Measuring Investor Sentiment with Mutual Fund Flows," *Journal of Finance Economics* 104, no. 2 (2011): 363–382.

27. Nai-Fu Chen, Raymond Kan, and Merton H. Miller, "Are the Discounts on Closed-End Funds a Sentiment Index," *Journal of Finance* 48, no. 2 (1993): 795–800.

28. Navin Chopra, Charles M. C. Lee, Andrei Shleifer, and Richard H. Thaler, "Yes, Discounts on Closed-End Funds Are a Sentiment Index," *Journal of Finance* 48, no. 2 (1993): 801–808.
29. David Rapach, Matthew Ringgenberg, and Guofu Zhou, "Short Interest and Aggregate Market Returns," WFA—Center for Finance and Accounting Research Working Paper, No. 14/002, 2014.
30. Kenneth R. French, G. William Schwert, and Robert F. Stambaugh, "Expected Stock Returns and Volatility," *Journal of Financial Economics* 19 (1987): 3–29.
31. Yigit Atilgan, Turan G. Bali, and K. Ozgur Demirtas, "Implied Volatility Spreads and Expected Market Returns," *Journal of Business & Economic Statistics* (2014).
32. Turan G. Bali and Armen Hovakimian, "Volatility Spreads and Expected Stock Returns," *Management Science* 55 (2009): 1797–1812.
33. Tim Bollerslev, George Tauchen, and Hao Zhou, "Expected Stock Return and Variance Risk Premia," *Review of Financial Studies* 22, no. 11 (2009): 4463–4492.
34. Maggie M. Copeland and Thomas E. Copeland, "Market Timing: Style and Size Rotation Using the VIX," *Financial Analysts Journal* 55, no. 2 (1999): 73–81.
35. Bryan Kelly and Hao Jiang, "Tail Risk and Asset Prices," *Review of Financial Studies* (2014).
36. Christopher J. Neely, David E. Rapach, Jun Tu, and Zhou, "Forecasting the Equity Risk Premium: The Role of Technical Indicators," *Management Science* 60, no. 7 (2014): 1772–1791.
37. David Rapach and Guofu Zhou, "Forecasting Stock Returns." In *Handbook of Economic Forecasting*, vol. 2, ed. Graham Elliott and Allen Timmermann (Amsterdam: Elsevier, 2013), p. 329.

CHAPTER 8

Simple Security Selection Models That Work

"At least 316 factors have been tested to explain the cross-section of expected returns ... Given the plethora of factors and the inevitable data mining, many of the historically discovered factors would be deemed "significant" by chance."
—Harvey, Liu, and Zhu (2014)[1]

The search for an edge in the markets is endless. There are now hundreds of papers claiming to have found anomalous returns (i.e., anomalies). The quote above is from a 2014 paper by professors Harvey, Liu, and Zhu from Duke and Texas A&M, who examine 316 "anomalous" factors. Their conclusion is that "most claimed research findings in financial economics are likely false." However, some anomalies still pass the high hurdles for success outlined in the Harvey, Liu, and Zhu research article.

Only two factors are both statistically reliable *and* simple to implement by a do-it-yourself investor. These two factors are value and momentum. As evidenced in Fama and French's 2012 paper, "Size, Value, and Momentum in International Stock Returns," value and momentum work across all markets.[2] So we will all be billionaires, right? Not so fast. Let's walk through why the market anomalies exist and what traits an investor must have to exploit them.

VALUE INVESTING

Value investing has been discussed for decades and was originally outlined in *Security Analysis* by Graham and Dodd in 1934.[3] One of Ben Graham's best students, Warren Buffett, is widely followed by the media and has built his personal wealth through his company Berkshire Hathaway. The story is simple: Buy stocks at less than their intrinsic value. Since many people take pride in being frugal and getting a great deal, value investing is intuitive and has developed into a religion with a cult-like following.

The story behind value-investing is intuitive, but what is the evidence to support the argument that buying cheap stocks outperforms the market? Academia has been studying this question for decades, and the data to verify the research behind value-investing are publicly available: Ken French, an esteemed finance professor at Dartmouth, makes available a compilation of data through his website.[4] French's value portfolios are formed by taking the universe of US stocks, and splitting the universe into 10 portfolios (deciles) on June 30 each year based on each firm's book-to-market ratio. The book-to-market ratio (B/M) is simply the firm's book value of assets divided by its market capitalization. This ratio compares the value of the assets (book) to the price one would pay for the assets. Those firms with higher B/M values are considered to be cheap, or "value" stocks, while firms with lower B/M values are expensive, or "growth" stocks. The B/M ratio is similar to the commonly used earnings-to-price (E/P) ratio. Eugene Fama and Ken French consider B/M a superior metric for the following reason:

> We always emphasize that different price ratios are just different ways to scale a stock's price with a fundamental, to extract the information in the cross-section of stock prices about expected returns. One fundamental (book value, earnings, or cashflow) is pretty much as good as another for this job, and the average return spreads produced by different ratios are similar to and, in statistical terms, indistinguishable from one another. We like BtM because the book value in the numerator is more stable over time than earnings or cashflow, which is important for keeping turnover down in a value portfolio.[5]

The summary statistics for returns associated with B/M portfolios from January 1, 1927, to December 31, 2014, are presented in Table 8.1. The results are for value-weighted portfolios to the top decile formed on B/M (value stocks) and the bottom decile formed on B/M (growth stocks) using Ken French's data. To illustrate how these portfolios are formed, if there are a thousand stocks in the universe, 100 stocks would go into each

TABLE 8.1 Value and Growth Stocks Summary Statistics

	Value Firms VW	Growth Firms VW	US Bonds	SP500
CAGR	12.40%	8.68%	5.45%	9.95%
Standard Deviation	31.92%	19.94%	6.92%	19.09%
Downside Deviation	21.35%	14.41%	4.43%	14.22%
Sharpe Ratio	0.41	0.35	0.31	0.41
Sortino Ratio (MAR = 5%)	0.54	0.37	0.12	0.45
Worst Drawdown	−91.67%	−85.01%	−20.97%	−84.59%

B/M decile, and these 100 stocks would be value-weighted, or weighted by their market capitalization among the 100 stocks in a given portfolio. The portfolios are rebalanced every June 30 and the portfolio performance is recorded.

The evidence is clear: Value stocks have outperformed the market and growth firms since 1927. The compound annual growth rate (CAGR) for value firms is 12.40 percent, while growth firms earned a return of 8.68 percent. The comparison benchmark, the S&P 500, earned 9.95 percent over the same time period, while investing in US 10-year bonds yielded a total return of 5.45 percent.

But why have value stocks outperformed? There are two main theories for why value investing has worked in the past. The first theory, argued by Fama and French in their 1993 paper, "Common Risk Factors in the Returns on Stocks and Bonds," is that low book-to-market (B/M), or value stocks, earn a higher average return as compensation for risk.[6] Their finding is that stocks move well with the market, but to the extent there is cross-section variation in returns, this is driven by variation in size and value factors. Simply put, their theory is that value stocks are riskier, so their expected returns should be higher. The second theory, originally proposed by Warren Buffett's teacher, Ben Graham, and formally investigated in a 1994 paper by Lakonishok, Shleifer, and Vishny (LSV), is that value stocks earn higher returns because investors make behavioral errors and push stocks beyond their intrinsic value.[7] The bias LSV describe is referred to as representative bias, where investors naively extrapolate past growth rates into the future.

Figure 8.1 is created from data in the Dechow and Sloan 1997 paper, converted from Table 1 in their paper, to a bar graph for expositional purposes to highlight the concept outlined in the LSV 1994 paper.

The picture in Figure 8.1 splits firms into 10 portfolios based on their book-to-market ratio. The far left bucket contains the most expensive firms (growth firms), while the far right bucket contains the cheapest

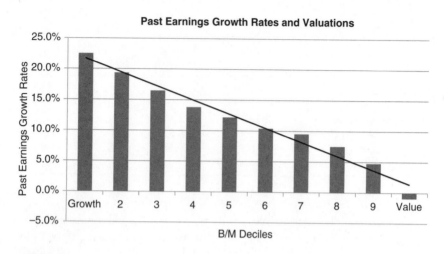

FIGURE 8.1 Past 5-Year Earnings Growth Rates and Prices

firms (value firms). The gray bars represent past earning growth rates over 5 years. There is a clear linear relationship between price and past growth rates: Higher prices are associated with higher past growth rates. Investors see these past growth rates and extrapolate them into the future, which is why growth stocks are expensive and why value stocks are cheap. However, *investors fail to account for mean reversion in future earnings growth rates*: High past growth rates end up lower in the future than they have been in the past and low past growth rates end up higher in the future than they have been in the past.

Figure 8.2 takes the same 10 portfolios from Figure 8.1 and examines these portfolios' realized *future* 5-year earnings growth rates. Note the mean reversion—growth rates are all similar across the valuation buckets. Value outperforms growth because expensive securities have realized growth rates that are lower than expectation, while cheap securities have higher than expected growth rates. The market is consistently—and predictably— surprised by mean-reversion in earnings growth. As long as investors suffer from representative bias, and continue to extrapolate past performance into the future—failing to account for mean-reversion—there will be a predictable spread in the returns between value and growth stocks due to mispricing and not due to differences in risk between value and growth firms.

We would be remiss if we did not mention the key finding by Dechow and Sloan in 1997,[8] who take the LSV analysis one step further. Dechow and Sloan argue that the value premium isn't driven by naïve extrapolation of past fundamental performance metrics, but instead, the value premium is

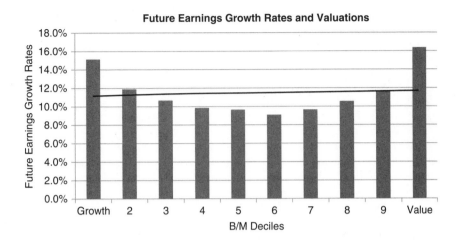

FIGURE 8.2 Future 5-Year Earnings Growth Rates

caused by a naïve reliance on analysts' forecasted earnings growth. In other words: avoid sell-side analyst forecasts. Analysts, like other humans, suffer from representative bias, and extrapolate past earnings growth rates too far into the future. Regardless of the nuanced arguments among the behavioral camp, the point is clear: Excess returns associated with value stocks appear to be driven by mispricing due to human bias.

A Simple Value Model that Works

Value investing has worked over a long period of time, and the foundation for the excess returns associated with cheap stocks is likely due to human behavioral bias. To exploit this anomaly as a DIY investor, we need to identify the best methodology, but also keep things simple. To identify the best method we examine three commonly used valuation measures.

- B/M
- E/P
- EBIT/TEV

The first measure is the book-to-market (B/M) ratio which is commonly used in academic research, as discussed earlier. A common practitioner ratio is the price-to-earnings (P/E) ratio. This metric simply takes the price of the stock and divides it by the earnings per share of the firm. For comparison's sake, we use the inverse of this ratio, or the earnings-to-price (E/P) ratio. The last measure we examine is earnings before interest and taxes divided by the total enterprise value (EBIT/TEV). This measures how much operating profit a firm makes (EBIT) and divides it by the total amount one would need to pay to buy the entire firm (TEV). The TEV measure is the sum of the firm's market capitalization (stock), debt and preferred stock, minus the firm's cash value. This measure is commonly used by private equity firms to ascertain the costs of purchasing all assets of a firm. The TEV measure helps private equity firms compare publically traded firms with different capital structures.

Stock returns are measured from July 1, 1963, through December 31, 2014 (we do not have reliable data prior to 1963). We eliminate smaller firms based on the NYSE market capitalization breakpoints. Specifically, we eliminate any firms below the NYSE 40th percentile for market capitalization. As of December 31, 2014, this was around $1.9 billion. We do this to examine mid- to large-cap firms and to minimize erroneous results associated with micro-cap or small-cap firms. Firms are sorted into deciles on each valuation measure (i.e., B/M, E/P, or EBIT/TEV) on June 30 of year t, and this value is used to compute the monthly returns from July 1 of year t to June 30 of year t +1. Last, we require firms to include each of the three ratios in the universe of stocks under analysis.

Results are shown for the top decile (Panel A: value stocks), bottom decile (Panel B: growth stocks), as well the universe of firms from which we select. All portfolios are market-cap weighted (see Table 8.2).[9]

Over the 1963 through 2014 period analyzed, we find that EBIT/TEV is the best valuation metric to use as an investment strategy relative to other valuation metrics. Similar results are found using EBITDA/TEV in a 2009 paper by Loughran and Wellman,[10] as well as a 2012 paper by Gray and

TABLE 8.2 Valuation Horserace (7/1963–12/2014)

	Value-weight portfolios			
	B/M	E/P	EBIT/ TEV	VW Market
Panel A: Value Stocks				
CAGR	12.36%	13.52%	14.33%	10.14%
Sharpe Ratio	0.47	0.54	0.61	0.39
Sortino Ratio	0.63	0.74	0.86	0.53
Worst Drawdown	−68.16%	−55.80%	−42.85%	−50.87%
Panel B: Growth Stocks				
CAGR	8.49%	7.60%	6.08%	10.14%
Sharpe Ratio	0.26	0.22	0.17	0.39
Sortino Ratio	0.34	0.29	0.22	0.53
Worst Drawdown	−80.09%	−80.82%	−89.92%	−50.87%

Vogel.[11] The returns to an annually rebalanced value-weight portfolio of high EBIT/TEV stocks, earn 14.33 percent a year. This compares favorably to a practitioner favorite, E/P and the academic favorite B/M. Cheap E/P stocks earn 13.52 percent a year, while the academic favorite (B/M) earns 12.36 percent.

We also examine the return spread between the value and growth firms, and find that EBIT/TEV yields the largest return difference of the three measures. The bigger the spread, the better job the valuation measure does at differentiating between stocks that are statistically likely to outperform and those likely to underperform. When comparing the Sharpe ratio and Sortino ratio, EBIT/TEV wins again. These ratios attempt to compare risk-adjusted performance, with higher values being preferred. Last, EBIT/TEV has lower drawdowns for value stocks compared to the other measures. The conclusions are similar when looking at portfolios that are equal-weighted and value-weighted.

Overall, it appears that using EBIT/TEV was the best way to form a portfolio of value securities from 1963 to 2014. However, all three measures are effective relative to buying and holding the market portfolio.

Valuation metrics that incorporate last year's earnings are interesting, but what about *long-term* valuation metrics? Going back to the 1930s, practitioners have promoted the concept of using normalized earnings in place of simple one-year earnings estimates. For example, Graham and Dodd refer to the use of current earnings in the context of valuation metrics: "[earnings in P/E] should cover a period of not less than five years, and preferably seven to ten years."[12] More recently, academics such as Campbell and Shiller, suggest that annual earnings are noisy as a measure of fundamental value.[13]

Here we test this theory by examining the three measures with long-term valuation metrics. Specifically, the central hypothesis proposed by proponents of long-term valuation metrics is that "normalizing" earnings decreases the noise of the valuation signal and therefore increases the predictive power of the metric. In the case of EBIT/TEV, this is represented by the following equation:

$$EBIT/TEV_{n,i} = \frac{\frac{\sum_{j=1}^{n} EBIT_{ij}}{n}}{TEV_i}$$

We test this conjecture and highlight the results in Table 8.3. In each column, we represent a different perturbation of the long-term valuation metric. For example, the two-year column uses the two-year average of the numerator for the valuation metric. Note that the results run from July 1, 1971, until December 31, 2014, as we require firms to have eight years of data to be in the sample. The results shown are for value-weighted portfolios.

TABLE 8.3 Long-Term Valuation Horserace

Value-Weight	VW Value							
	1yr	2yr	3yr	4yr	5yr	6yr	7yr	8yr
B/M	14.92%	15.00%	14.85%	15.02%	15.15%	15.38%	15.43%	15.54%
E/P	14.86%	14.81%	15.16%	14.62%	14.68%	15.02%	15.07%	14.90%
EBIT/TEV	15.62%	15.27%	14.84%	14.73%	14.83%	14.76%	14.71%	14.66%
	VW Growth							
B/M	10.73%	10.86%	10.62%	10.33%	10.03%	9.84%	9.81%	9.54%
E/P	9.98%	10.88%	11.07%	11.44%	11.04%	10.91%	11.04%	10.53%
EBIT/TEV	8.43%	9.51%	9.26%	9.55%	9.60%	9.09%	9.23%	9.13%
	Spread (Value-Growth)							
B/M	4.18%	4.14%	4.23%	4.69%	5.11%	5.53%	5.62%	6.00%
E/P	4.88%	3.93%	4.09%	3.17%	3.64%	4.11%	4.03%	4.37%
EBIT/TEV	7.20%	5.77%	5.58%	5.17%	5.22%	5.67%	5.48%	5.53%

As we can see from Table 8.3, it does not appear that using long-term valuation metrics adds value, on average. Examining the spread between value and growth firms, it appears that long-term measures work well for the B/M measure, as the spread between value and growth gets larger as more years of data are used. However, the difference in the value stocks for the B/M measure only increases by 0.62 percent, from 14.92 percent to 15.54 percent. Comparing the other two measures, there does not appear to be any benefit from using long-term valuation metrics. For the E/P measure, the spread between value and growth does not increase as more years are used, and for the EBIT/TEV measure, the spread actually decreases as more years are used. Examining the value stock portfolios by themselves, the best performing EBIT/TEV portfolio only includes one year of data! Thus, we think that sorting stocks on EBIT/TEV is a simple and effective way to capture the value premium.

MOMENTUM INVESTING

As many investors know, Eugene Fama developed the efficient-market hypothesis (EMH) at the University of Chicago in the 1960s and 1970s, and it subsequently flourished across academia.[14] Under the strong-form interpretation of the EMH, asset prices reflect all available information (public and private), and there is no way for investors to consistently outperform a randomly selected basket of securities after controlling for risk. As noted EMH proponent Burton Malkiel so eloquently put it in his

1973 classic, *A Random Walk Down Wall Street*: "A blindfolded monkey throwing darts at a newspaper's financial pages could select a portfolio that would do just as well as one carefully selected by experts."[15]

Indeed, the cult of efficient markets was pervasive in many of the nation's business schools, and heretics have been frequently banished from the EMH temple. While some finance professors openly scoffed at the notion of being able to add value through fundamental analysis, they reserved the innermost concentric circle of hell for technical analysts, who were perceived as financial quacks and charlatans. Why? Because Wall Street is a random walk, and past price movements tell you nothing about the future.

Yet all was not well in EMH paradise, as it emerged there was more to the story. Anomalies that were inconsistent with EMH began to emerge in the literature in the 1970s—for example, as was mentioned in the previous section, Ben Graham showed that buying a basket of low P/E stocks tends to outperform the market. At around the same time that the EMH was basking in glory, Daniel Kahneman, working with Amos Tversky, started exploring cognitive and behavioral psychology and how our biases affect individual financial decision-making. Kahneman and Tversky established a connection between investors' internal behavioral biases and many of the observed anomalies that were being identified in academic finance literature.

In the early 1990s, academics such as Narasimhan Jagadeesh and Sheridan Titman, in their 1993 paper "Returns to Buying Winners and Selling Losers: Implications for Market Efficiency," began to focus on the concept of *momentum*, which refers to the fact that, in direct contradiction to the EMH, past returns can predict future returns.[16] That is, if a stock has performed well over the past year, it will continue to perform well in the future. EMH proponents were perplexed by the momentum anomaly, but argued that momentum returns were likely related to additional risks borne: riskier smaller and cheaper companies drove the effect. Many researchers have responded with studies that find the effect persists even when controlling for company size and value factors. And the effect appears to hold across multiple asset classes, such as commodities, currencies, and even bonds.[17]

In short, it appears the evidence for momentum is best described by the strongest supporters of EMH. Eugene Fama and Ken French, in their 2008 paper, "Dissecting Anomalies," state that momentum is "pervasive."[18] Today, researchers are going even further by applying behavioral finance concepts in order to understand psychological factors that drive the momentum effect. In "Demystifying Managed Futures," Brian Hurst, Yao Hua Ooi, and Lasse Heje Pedersen argue that the returns for even the largest and most successful managed futures funds and CTAs can be attributed to momentum strategies.[19] They also discuss a model for the lifecycle of a trend, and then draw on behavioral psychology to hypothesize the cognitive mechanisms

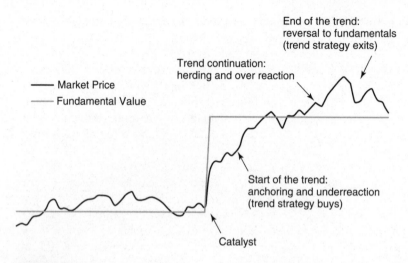

FIGURE 8.3 Lifecycle of a Trend

that drive the underlying momentum effect. Figure 8.3 shows a graph from their paper of a typical trend.

Note that there are several distinct components to the trend: (1) initial underreaction, when market price is below fundamental value; (2) overreaction, as the market price exceeds fundamental value, and (3) the end of the trend, when the price converges with fundamental value. There are several behavioral biases that may systematically contribute to these components.

Underreaction Phase

Adjustment and Anchoring

- This occurs when we consider a value for a quantity before estimating that quantity. Consider the following two questions posed by Kahneman: Was Gandhi more or less than 144 years old when he died? How old was Gandhi when he died? Your guess was affected by the suggestion of his advanced age, which led you to anchor on it and then insufficiently adjust from that starting point, similar to how people underreact to news about a security. (Gandhi died at 79.)

The Disposition Effect

- This is the tendency of investors to sell their winners too early and hold on to losers too long. Selling early creates selling pressure on winner stocks in the underreaction phase, and reduces selling pressure on losing stocks in the underreaction phase, thus delaying the price discovery process in both cases.

Overreaction Phase

Feedback Trading and the Herd Effect

- Traders follow positive feedback strategies. For instance, George Soros has described his concept of reflexivity, which can involve buying in anticipation of further buying by uninformed investors in a self-reinforcing process. Additionally, herding can be a defense mechanism occurring when an animal reduces its risk of being eaten by a predator by staying with the crowd. As Charles MacKay put it in 1841 in his book *Extraordinary Popular Delusions and Madness of Crowds*, "Men, it has been well said, think in herds; it will be seen that they go mad in herds, while they only recover their senses slowly, and one by one."[20]

Confirmation Bias and Representativeness

- In general, we suffer from a bias to confirm our beliefs and tend to search for information that supports those beliefs. Such a biased view might cause investors to move more money into investments, supporting a trend, when a dispassionate appraisal might suggests price already exceeds fundamental value. Similarly, investors see recent price momentum and assume via representativeness that this reflects future conditions, likewise supporting the trend.

We found that the trend lifecycle framework and proposed underlying psychological factors made good intuitive sense and were consistent with both the momentum effect itself as well as many established behavioral finance concepts.

The growing academic body of work supporting the existence of the momentum effect, along with a sensible psychological framework that explains it, are a potent combination. Indeed, momentum has been labeled by Eugene Fama, winner of the 2013 Nobel Prize in Economics and king of the efficient market hypothesis, as "the premier anomaly."[21]

Does Momentum Work?

Momentum investing may sound preposterous to those who believe in efficient markets. The idea is simple: Each month, rank stocks on past prices and buy the top decile of firms that have performed the best over the past 12 months. The summary statistics for momentum portfolio returns for all US stocks (using Ken French's data) from January 1, 1927, to December 31, 2014, are presented in Table 8.4. We show the results of value-weighted portfolios to the top decile formed on momentum (2- to 12-month look-back) and the bottom decile formed on momentum (2- to 12-month look-back).

TABLE 8.4   High and Low Momentum

	High Mom VW	Low Mom VW	US Bonds	SP500
CAGR	16.92%	−1.51%	5.45%	9.95%
Standard Deviation	22.58%	33.94%	6.92%	19.09%
Downside Deviation	16.70%	21.97%	4.43%	14.22%
Sharpe Ratio	0.66	0.01	0.31	0.41
Sortino Ratio (MAR = 5%)	0.80	-0.05	0.12	0.45
Worst Drawdown	−76.29%	−96.95%	−20.97%	−84.59%
Worst Month Return	−28.52%	−42.26%	−8.41%	−28.73%
Best Month Return	28.88%	93.98%	15.23%	41.65%
Profitable Months	63.16%	51.42%	63.35%	61.74%
Cumulative Draw Downs	−32404.12%	−49253.34%	−8237.57%	−28514.52%

Wow! That has always been our first reaction to these results. Again, one does not need any financial statement data to construct these portfolios, just past prices. The spread between high and low momentum stocks from 1927 to 2014 was *18.43 percent*. This is close to five times the spread between value and growth firms (3.72% over the same time period) as shown above. Additionally, the top momentum stocks outperformed the S&P 500 by 6.97 percent. Christopher Geczy and Mikhail Samonov examine a momentum strategy over an even longer period in an aptly named paper, "212 Years of Price Momentum (The World's Longest Backtest: 1801–2012)," and find that momentum has worked for over 200 years.[22]

Although momentum investment strategies are well known in academic literature, these strategies are not commonly used in actively managed funds. Most mutual fund complexes split the universe into value and growth stocks. To highlight this framework in the marketplace, we post a screenshot from Vanguard's website, which splits the universe into nine buckets. The two axes are market cap (vertical axis, from small to large) and style (horizontal axis, which goes from value to growth).

A chart like Figure 8.4 is used by almost every major investment firm in the United States. We talked in the last section about how value stocks outperform growth stocks, and showed that buying and holding growth stocks is a terrible bet. Most people's immediate gut reaction to "momentum" is that momentum investing *IS* growth investing. Unfortunately, this is a misconception in the market. Momentum and growth, while related, are certainly not the same. We explore some data to flesh out this point. We examine

Vanguard 500 Index Fund Investor Shares (VFINX)

Also available as a lower-cost Admiral™ Shares mutual fund and an ETF.

BUY   COMPARE   ADD TO WATCH LIST

Overview   Price & Performance   Portfolio & Management   Fees & Minimums   Distributions   News & Reviews

Portfolio

Stock style

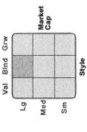

Vanguard 500 Index Fund seeks to track the performance of a benchmark index that measures the investment return of large-capitalization stocks.

Learn more about this portfolio's investment strategy and policy.

FIGURE 8.4 Vanguard Stock Style Chart

data from July 1, 1963, until December 31, 2014, and explore the over-lap between the top decile of mid to large cap stocks formed on past 2- to 12-month momentum and a decile of growth stocks (formed on EBIT/TEV). We find that the overlap between the portfolios is only 29 percent! So while momentum and growth are considered similar by the ill-informed investment community, they are decidedly *not the same.*

Overall, we believe that human behavioral biases cause a systematic momentum premium. The goal of the next section is to explain how an investor can construct a simple security selection momentum model.

A SIMPLE MOMENTUM MODEL THAT WORKS

How does one go about implementing a momentum strategy? The ways portfolios are formed in academic literature vary. However, there is one recurring theme: All momentum strategies sort stocks based on past returns (generally 6 to 12 months of past cumulative returns). Screening securities based on this metric is relatively simple to accomplish. But how does a simple momentum model perform? Similar to value, we examine only firms above the NYSE 40th percentile for market capitalization to eliminate smaller firms and minimize the size effect. Portfolios are formed by equally weighting the firms.

The way in which we choose to implement a simple momentum strat-egy is as follows: Calculate the cumulative returns to stocks over the past 12 months, ignoring the last month. We ignore the last month to exploit the empirical finding that there is a negative correlation of month-to-month returns (reversal rather than continuation).[23] Next, we sort stocks based on their cumulative 2- to 12-month past returns, and buy an equal-weighted basket of stocks from the top decile. We repeat this process each month.

Here is a simple series of returns to illustrate how to calculate the cumu-lative returns. To calculate the cumulative returns over the past 12 months (ignoring the last month), we take the return stream and adds 1. Then, we multiply the series of (1 + return) and subtract 1. So the cumulative returns in December (momentum score) is calculated as follows:

$$(1.01)(1.02)(0.99)(1.01)(0.98)(1.05)(1.00)(1.01)(0.97)(1.04)(1.02)-1$$

$$= 9.07\%$$

Notice that we ignore the returns from December (−1.00%) when calculating the momentum score at the end of December (see Table 8.5). We simply need to do this for all stocks—buy the top decile, and repeat each month. If eliminating the last month is too difficult to implement for the DIY

TABLE 8.5 Simple Momentum Example

	Stock Returns	1+Return	Momentum
January	1.00%	1.01	
February	2.00%	1.02	
March	−1.00%	0.99	
April	0.50%	1.01	
May	−2.00%	0.98	
June	5.00%	1.05	
July	−0.50%	1.00	
August	1.00%	1.01	
September	−3.00%	0.97	
October	4.00%	1.04	
November	2.00%	1.02	
December	−1.00%	0.99	9.07%

investor, it is not going to destroy the benefits of the momentum strategy if a DIY investor simply ranks stocks on the past one-year cumulative returns.

Momentum sounds too good to be true. What's the catch? One issue is that trading costs can negatively affect momentum strategies, as pointed out by Lesmond, Schill, and Zhou. An investor in momentum strategies should expect to lose around 2.40 percent per year (0.20 percent per month) due to the frequent rebalancing required.[24] When faced with these trading costs, as well as high short-term capital gain rates, the benefits of a momentum strategy quickly evaporate. A common solution to the trading and tax costs is to propose a less-frequent rebalance interval of one year. Unfortunately, in contrast to value strategies, momentum strategies lose most of their edge if they are not rebalanced frequently.

Table 8.6 shows the results from January 1, 1927, until December 31, 2014, when varying the holding periods. When holding firms for over a month, we form overlapping portfolios. An example of a 3-month hold portfolio would be as follows: on January 1, buy the top decile and hold until March 31; on February 1, buy the top decile and hold until April 30; on March 1, buy the top decile and hold until May 31. So the portfolio return during March would be the equal-weighted basket of the stocks added on January 1, February 1, and March 1.

The results shown are equal-weighted returns from January 1, 1927, to December 31, 2014, for firms above the 40th percentile for NYSE market capitalization. The spread between the top and bottom decile monotonically decreases as the holding period increases. The spread between high and low momentum goes from 17.49 percent for a 1-month holding period to only 5.49 percent if one holds for 12 months. Additionally, what is the

TABLE 8.6   Equal Weighted Returns across Varying Hold Periods

	Decile 1	Decile 10	Spread (10-1)	EW Universe	Decile 10–Universe
1 M hold	1.54%	19.03%	17.49%	11.19%	7.84%
2 M hold	2.19%	18.57%	16.38%	11.19%	7.37%
3 M hold	2.82%	17.66%	14.84%	11.19%	6.47%
4 M hold	3.35%	17.01%	13.65%	11.19%	5.81%
5 M hold	3.74%	16.57%	12.83%	11.19%	5.38%
6 M hold	4.20%	16.00%	11.80%	11.19%	4.81%
7 M hold	4.68%	15.52%	10.84%	11.19%	4.32%
8 M hold	5.18%	15.00%	9.82%	11.19%	3.80%
9 M hold	5.67%	14.36%	8.69%	11.19%	3.17%
10 M hold	6.13%	13.81%	7.68%	11.19%	2.62%
11 M hold	6.60%	13.25%	6.65%	11.19%	2.06%
12 M hold	7.18%	12.67%	5.49%	11.19%	1.48%

value-add of a long-only momentum strategy relative to an equal-weighted universe that is not sorted based on momentum criteria? For portfolios with a 1-month hold, the value add of long-only momentum over the equal-weighted universe is 7.84 percent for a 1-month hold, while the value add of long-only momentum for a 12-month hold is only 1.48 percent.

The previous results suggest that we rebalance the momentum portfolio each month. Momentum profits are larger at a more frequent rebalance period: Even if one subtracts 2.40 percent due to transaction costs, the value-add of long-only momentum over an equal-weight universe for a 1-month hold is still 5.44 percent per year, after deducting these transaction costs. The only other obstacle to a successful momentum strategy is taxes, but one can attempt to minimize this by allocating to momentum in a tax-deferred account (IRA, 401(k)) or through a momentum exchange-traded fund (ETF).

COMBINING VALUE AND MOMENTUM

Our prior analysis supports the notion that simple value and simple momentum models can be effective security selection tools. But what happens when we combine these two security selection procedures? We test the following strategy from July 1, 1963, through December 31, 2014: The Simple Value portfolio is formed on July 1 of year t and held until June 30 of year t +1. This portfolio is an equal-weight portfolio of the top decile of firms formed on EBIT/TEV. The Simple MOM portfolio is formed at a monthly frequency. We form portfolios of firms above the NYSE 40th percentile for market capitalization to avoid issues associated with micro and small-cap stocks (as of December 31, 2014, the minimum size company would be $1.9 billion). The assumption is to buy at the close on the last day of the month, and hold until the close of the last day of the month. This portfolio is formed by buying the top decile of firms formed on their cumulative returns over the past 12 months, ignoring the last month.

We also show the returns to a portfolio, which allocates 50 percent to Simple Value, and 50 percent to Simple MOM. The assumption is that the allocation between the Value and Momentum portfolios is reset to 50/50 at the end of each month. Table 8.7 shows the returns for the portfolios described.

As one can see from the results, both the Simple Value and Simple MOM portfolios outperform the market. Both have higher CAGRs and Sharpe and Sortino ratios than the market. However, momentum does have a larger drawdown than the S&P 500. Examining the combination of 50 percent value and 50 percent momentum, this portfolio generates even higher Sharpe and Sortino ratios, with a lower drawdown than the market. The correlation between value and momentum is only 68.60 percent, which is much lower than the correlation between value and the S&P 500 (87.54%) and the correlation between momentum and the S&P 500 (74.15%). This lower correlation gives some diversification benefits when combining the two portfolios. Overall, the 50 percent value and 50 percent momentum portfolio outperforms the market, as it beats the S&P 500 100.00 percent across 10-year rolling periods.

Table 8.8 provides the annual returns to the four portfolios.

TABLE 8.7 Simple Value and Momentum Annual Results

	50% Value, 50% MOM	Simple Value	Simple MOM	SP500
CAGR	17.72%	15.69%	18.86%	10.23%
Standard Deviation	19.46%	17.48%	24.79%	14.86%
Downside Deviation	13.80%	12.64%	17.35%	10.60%
Sharpe Ratio	0.69	0.65	0.63	0.40
Sortino Ratio (MAR = 5%)	0.97	0.89	0.89	0.56
Worst Drawdown	−50.18%	−47.33%	−58.40%	−50.21%
Worst Month Return	−25.85%	−20.96%	−30.74%	−21.58%
Best Month Return	20.82%	25.43%	42.73%	16.81%
Profitable Months	62.62%	62.30%	62.94%	61.65%
Cumulative Draw Downs	−15504.56%	−14806.83%	−19368.90%	−14818.19%

TABLE 8.8 Simple Value and Momentum Annual Returns

	50% Value, 50% MOM	Simple Value	Simple MOM	SP500
1963	9.08%	4.96%	13.27%	10.00%
1964	20.52%	20.18%	20.74%	16.67%
1965	45.71%	28.55%	64.51%	12.61%
1966	−0.36%	−9.11%	8.04%	−10.20%
1967	58.44%	45.99%	71.35%	23.97%
1968	30.17%	31.43%	28.11%	10.84%
1969	−10.96%	−16.83%	−5.12%	−8.31%
1970	−0.23%	12.37%	−12.03%	4.00%
1971	25.87%	14.34%	38.12%	14.45%
1972	18.14%	9.45%	26.96%	19.11%
1973	−12.75%	−24.53%	0.04%	−14.81%
1974	−24.65%	−21.31%	−28.27%	−26.42%
1975	53.93%	62.25%	45.51%	36.95%
1976	45.13%	51.86%	38.62%	23.92%
1977	13.75%	11.61%	15.81%	-7.43%
1978	15.79%	9.38%	21.97%	6.40%
1979	51.14%	39.45%	63.36%	18.60%
1980	46.64%	22.13%	73.53%	32.60%
1981	−2.67%	6.24%	−11.47%	−4.88%
1982	30.99%	21.21%	41.22%	22.15%
1983	28.45%	34.99%	21.27%	22.30%
1984	3.01%	11.59%	-5.28%	6.69%
1985	33.83%	31.03%	36.58%	32.01%
1986	19.47%	21.38%	17.07%	18.07%
1987	10.50%	7.37%	12.78%	5.15%
1988	22.18%	29.23%	15.02%	16.95%
1989	29.85%	23.48%	36.33%	31.39%
1990	−12.57%	−14.35%	−10.94%	−3.20%
1991	62.88%	42.58%	85.27%	30.68%
1992	21.10%	23.36%	18.66%	7.73%
1993	24.59%	13.91%	35.64%	9.89%
1994	−0.16%	1.08%	−1.59%	1.35%
1995	38.95%	28.46%	49.48%	37.64%
1996	24.03%	27.45%	19.76%	23.23%
1997	23.31%	34.93%	12.02%	33.60%
1998	13.43%	1.30%	25.70%	29.32%
1999	60.72%	1.79%	144.85%	21.35%
2000	10.14%	31.13%	−19.44%	−8.34%
2001	0.48%	10.15%	−8.79%	−11.88%
2002	−9.72%	−8.00%	−11.69%	−21.78%
2003	49.79%	52.68%	46.70%	28.72%
2004	21.29%	29.35%	13.09%	10.98%

(continued)

TABLE 8.8   (*Continued*)

	50% Value, 50% MOM	Simple Value	Simple MOM	SP500
2005	22.91%	24.61%	21.11%	5.23%
2006	15.47%	18.13%	12.51%	15.69%
2007	16.92%	6.42%	28.11%	5.76%
2008	−34.91%	−26.23%	−43.42%	−36.46%
2009	20.07%	33.50%	7.37%	26.49%
2010	25.27%	19.30%	31.26%	15.35%
2011	−4.12%	−3.89%	−4.56%	2.11%
2012	20.60%	19.37%	21.73%	16.00%
2013	42.77%	42.86%	42.57%	32.39%
2014	4.46%	9.18%	−0.43%	13.69%

The annual returns highlight the unique benefit of combining value and momentum portfolios. The best case study is the Internet bubble and its subsequent bursting. During the heart of the Internet bubble in 1998 and 1999, the annual returns to a Simple Value strategy were 1.30 percent and 1.79 percent, respectively. Simple Value wildly underperformed the S&P 500, which had returns of 29.32 percent and 21.35 percent over the same period. Alternatively, the Simple MOM portfolio yielded 25.70 percent and 144.85 percent over the same time period!

Fast forward to the bursting of the Internet bubble in 2000 and 2001.

The Simple Value strategy outperforms, by earning 31.13 percent and 10.15 percent in 2000 and 2001, while the S&P 500 earned −8.34 percent and −11.88 percent, and the Simple MOM earned −19.44 percent and −8.79 percent.

The Internet bubble provides one small example to justify the 50/50 allocation between value and momentum. We think this simple 50/50 allocation is a sensible way to invest and with a little effort, a DIY investor can employ value and momentum security selection to their advantage.

INTERNATIONAL STOCKS

As was shown above, combining Value and Momentum strategies has worked well for stocks in the United States. But how do similar strategies work for international stocks? We test the following strategy from January 1, 1992, through December 31, 2014: We form portfolios of firms above the NYSE 40th percentile for market capitalization in United States dollars. We limit stocks to those from EAFE countries, as this is representative of developed international stock markets. The Simple International Value portfolio is formed on January 1 of year *t* and held until December 31 of year *t*. This portfolio is an equal-weight portfolio of the top decile of firms formed on EBIT/TEV. The Simple International MOM portfolio is formed at a monthly frequency. The assumption is to buy at the close on the last day of the month, and hold until the close of the last day of the month. This portfolio is formed by buying the top decile of firms formed on their cumulative returns over the past 12 months, ignoring the last month.

We also show the returns to a portfolio, which allocates 50 percent to Simple International Value, and 50 percent to Simple International MOM. The assumption is that the allocation between the Value and Momentum portfolios is reset to 50/50 at the end of each month. Table 8.9 shows the returns for the portfolios described.

The results suggest that both the Simple International Value and Simple International MOM portfolios outperform the market. Both have higher CAGRs and Sharpe and Sortino ratios than the market. Examining the combination of 50 percent value and 50 percent momentum, this portfolio generates high Sharpe and Sortino ratios, with a lower drawdown than the market. The correlation between value and momentum is only 73.55 percent, which is much lower than the correlation between International Value and the EAFE Index (89.56 percent) and the correlation between International Momentum and the EAFE Index (78.89 percent). This lower correlation creates potential diversification benefits when combining the two portfolios. Overall, the 50 percent value and 50 percent momentum portfolio outperforms the international benchmark. So for investors who want international stock market exposure, capturing Value and Momentum seems like a smart approach, at least historically.

TABLE 8.9 Simple Value and Momentum Annual Results

	50% Int'l Value, 50% Int'l MOM	Simple Int'l Value	Simple Int'l MOM	EAFE
CAGR	11.88%	12.32%	10.92%	5.39%
Standard Deviation	17.14%	17.12%	19.66%	16.50%
Downside Deviation	13.11%	12.91%	15.06%	12.10%
Sharpe Ratio	0.59	0.61	0.49	0.24
Sortino Ratio (MAR = 5%)	0.59	0.63	0.49	0.14
Worst Drawdown	−54.80%	−55.71%	−55.26%	−56.68%
Worst Month Return	−21.86%	−23.05%	−20.67%	−20.18%
Best Month Return	13.13%	19.23%	16.33%	12.80%
Profitable Months	62.32%	64.13%	62.32%	58.70%
Cumulative Draw Downs	−6399.47%	−5835.56%	−8186.87%	−7521.85%

GET 'ER DONE

Here are the steps necessary to form the simple value and simple momentum portfolios.

Simple Value

1. Identify investable universe; we generally eliminate micro-cap firms.
2. Using the most recent financial data for each firm in the universe, calculate the following:
   (a) EBIT = Earnings before interest and taxes.
   (b) TEV = Total enterprise value. TEV is the sum of the firm's market capitalization (stock), debt, and preferred stock, minus the firm's cash value.
3. For all firms in the universe, calculate EBIT/TEV.
4. Rank all firms and buy the top decile. Equal weight the firms selected.
5. Rebalance *annually*.

Simple Momentum

1. Identify investable universe; we generally eliminate micro-cap firms.
2. For all firms in the universe, calculate the firm's cumulative return over the past 12 months, ignoring the return from the last month. This is the momentum variable.
3. Rank all firms on momentum, and buy the top decile. Equal weight the firms selected.
4. Rebalance *monthly*.

Allocation

1. At the end of each month, ensure allocation is 50 percent in Simple Value, and 50 percent in Simple Momentum.

An often-overlooked detail is that the value portfolio is formed annually, while the momentum portfolio is formed monthly. We provide tools for DIY investors to manage these portfolios at our website: AlphaArchitect.com. If readers are interested in learning more about systematic value strategies we encourage them to read Wes's book, *Quantitative Value*,[25] and for those interested in learning more about momentum strategies, we recommend readers review our numerous momentum-related posts offered on our web site, AlphaArchitect.com.

SUMMARY

There is a lot of research covering many anomalies, and in Chapter 8 we introduced two—value and momentum—that are especially powerful and practically implementable. Next, we reviewed statistics relating to value, compared various popular metrics, and concluded that EBIT/TEV appears to perform the best. We also examined the momentum anomaly, including some long-term statistics, and discussed how to implement a momentum strategy. We then showed that combining value and momentum can increase risk-adjusted returns. Finally, we offer a simple outline of how to implement the overall strategy.

NOTES

1. Harvey Campbell, Yan Liu, and Heqing Zhu, "... and the Cross-Section of Expected Returns," Duke Working Paper (February 3, 2015).
2. Eugene F. Fama and Kenneth R. French, 2012, "Size, Value, and Momentum in International Stock Returns," *Journal of Financial Economics* 105, no. 3 (2012): 457–472.
3. Benjamin Graham and David Dodd, *Security Analysis* (New York: McGraw-Hill, 1934).
4. Kenneth R. French, "Current Research Returns," Tuck School of Business at Dartmouth (January 2015), http://mba.tuck.dartmouth.edu/pages/faculty/ken .french/data_library.html.
5. "Q & A: Why Use Book Value to Sort Stocks?" Fama/French Forum (June 27, 2011), http://www.dimensional.com/famafrench/questions-answers/qa-why-use-book-value-to-sort-stocks.aspx.
6. Eugene F. Fama and Kenneth R. French, "Common Risk Factors in the Returns on Stocks and Bonds," *Journal of Financial Economics* 33 (1993): 3–56.
7. Josef Lakonishok, Andrei Shleifer, and Robert W. Vishny, "Contrarian Investment, Extraploation, and Risk," *Journal of Finance* 49, no. 5 (1994): 1541–1578.
8. Patricia M. Dechow and Richard G. Sloan, "Returns to Contrarian Investment Strategies: Tests of the Naïve Expectations Hypothesis," *Journal of Financial Economics* 43 (1997): 3–27.
9. Equal-weight results are quantitatively similar.
10. Tim Loughran and Jay Wellman, "New Evidence on the Relation between the Enterprise Multiple and Average Stock Returns," *Journal of Financial and Quantitative Analysis* 46, no. 6 (2012): 1629–1650.
11. Wesley R. Gray and Jack Vogel, "Analyzing Valuation Measures: A Performance Horse Race over the Past 40 Years," *Journal of Portfolio Management*, 39, no. 1 (2012): 112–121.
12. Ibid., p. 452.

13. John Y. Campbell and Robert J. Shiller, "Valuation Ratios and the Long-Run Stock Market Outlook," *Journal of Portfolio Management* 24, no. 2 (1998): 11–26.

14. Eugene Fama, "Efficient Capital Markets: A Review of Theory and Empirical Work," *Journal of Finance* 25, no. 2 (1970): 383–417.

15. Burton G. Malkiel, *A Random Walk Down Wall Street* (New York: Norton, 1973).

16. Narasimhan Jegadeesh and Sheridan Titman, "Returns to Buying Winners and Selling Losers: Implications for Stock Market Efficiency," *Journal of Finance* 48, no. 1 (1993): 65–91.

17. Clifford S. Asness, Tobias J. Moskowitz, and Lasse H. Pedersen, "Value and Momentum Everywhere," *Journal of Finance* 68, no. 3 (2013): 929–985.

18. Eugene F. Fama and Kenneth R. French, "Dissecting Anomalies," *Journal of Financial Economics* 63 (2008): 1653–1678.

19. Brian Hurst, Yao H. Ooi, and Lasse J. Pedersen, "Demystifying Managed Futures," *Journal of Investment Management* 11, no. 3 (2013): 42–58.

20. Charles Mackay, *Extraordinary Popular Delusions and the Madness of Crowds* (London: Richard Bentley, 1841).

21. Eugene F. Fama and Kenneth R. French, "Dissecting Anomalies," *Journal of Financial Economics* 63 (2008): 1653–1678.

22. Christopher Geczy and Mikhail Samonov, "212 Years of Price Momentum (The World's Longest Backtest: 1801–2012)," working paper, 2014.

23. Narasimhan Jegadeesh, "Evidence of Predicatable Behavior of Security Returns," *Journal of Finance* 45, no. 3 (1990): 881–898.

24. David A. Lesmond, Michael J. Schill, and Chunsheng Zhou, "The Illusory Nature of Momentum Profits," *Journal of Financial Economics* 71 (2004): 349–380.

25. Wesley Gray and Tobias Carlisle, *Quantitative Value* (New Jersey: John Wiley & Sons, 2012).

CHAPTER 9

The Do-It-Yourself (DIY) Solution

"Let every man divide his money into three parts, and invest a third in land, a third in business and a third let him keep by him in reserve."

—Talmud, c. 1200 BC–AD 500

What is your portfolio's mission? Wealth is often built by concentrated holdings in the form of hard work, a family business, or an entrepreneurial endeavor, but wealth is protected by diversification. Having a clear purpose is the most important step when it comes to portfolio management. If the purpose is to generate enormous returns, that requires one type of portfolio, but if the purpose is to preserve wealth, that requires a completely different portfolio. For most families, the mission for their portfolio should look similar to the following:

- *Purpose of the portfolio:* Preserve and compound wealth to assure financial security.
- *Return objective:* RF (10 yr) + 400 bps, after-tax, and after-fees.
  - *E.g.,* 10-year = 2% ➔ 6% nominal return objective.
- *Risk appetite:* As low as practical to achieve objective.

While there is no "one-size-fits-all" portfolio, a systematic framework for decision-making can help simplify the process and minimize human errors. For every allocation contemplated, and each strategy that needs to be critically assessed, the FACTS framework (consisting of Fees, Access, Complexity, Taxes, and Search) can be employed to clarify important considerations for the prospective investor. An in-depth look at the FACTS framework is in Chapter 5, and we provide a bullet-point summary of each factor below:

- Fees
- Access
- Complexity
- Taxes
- Search

The high-level summary from the FACTS framework is as follows: Create a portfolio that minimizes fees, increases access to your own capital (e.g., liquid investments), is easy to understand (low complexity), minimizes taxes, and minimizes manager search costs. Our goal is to propose a do-it-yourself portfolio solution that optimizes across all five key points.

How Can You Achieve Your Mission?

Many investors are faced with a fundamental problem: What should they do with their money? People usually pursue one of four broad solutions to this problem—each has costs and benefits:

1. Hire an expensive investment advisor that offers a limited value proposition (generally a bad idea, although quite common).
2. Hire an affordable advisor that delivers a strong value proposition (reasonable idea).
3. Hire a cheap robo-advisor that will deliver a generic, but reasonable value proposition (reasonable idea).
4. Do it yourself (reasonable idea).

We think diligent investors can successfully move down the do-it-yourself path when equipped with the tools and knowledge to move forward. There are a few critical areas to get familiar with, but once that's complete, DIY is perfectly viable for many. For those who are not comfortable with the DIY approach, we recommend approach option two or three, depending on personal preferences and circumstances.

"*But I want to be a DIY investor, so what do I do next?*"

- *Easiest solution:* Buy 50 percent BND; 50 percent VT (or your own special weights depending on your risk tolerance, individual circumstances). BND is the Vanguard Total Bond Market ETF, which costs 8bps; VT is the Vanguard Total World Stock ETF, which costs 18bps. Insanely cheap; insanely easy; throw away the key. Not an unreasonable approach.

■ *More complex solution:* Meb Faber and Eric Richardson in their book *The Ivy Portfolio* hint at a DIY model that utilizes a simple 10-month trend-following rule to run a risk-managed portfolio allocated across US equity, developed equity, REITs, commodities, and US Treasury bonds. These five asset classes are commonly referred to as the "Ivy 5," and we introduced this concept in Chapter 6.

The Ivy 5 solution is a reasonable solution for a do-it-yourself investor, but the live performance of this strategy has been underwhelming over the past five years (2009–2014). Moreover, this solution—while simple—is a little *too* simple. However, not all is lost—simple still is the key to success, we just need to incorporate some of the lessons we have learned from the previous chapters. We explore what we call the do-it-yourself (DIY) solution that enhances the Ivy 5 model in three ways:

1. We focus on the FACTS framework for our portfolio decisions.
2. We introduce security selection (value and momentum).
3. We enhance the risk-management system (using ROBUST).

The outcome of our robust solution is DIY. The DIY mission is to deliver a low-cost, low-complexity, high-liquidity, diversified, tax-efficient, risk-managed retirement portfolio that is *strong and effective in all or most situations and conditions.* The goal of DIY is a fully integrated retirement solution that a DIY investor can deploy on their own and with minimal interference from the "experts."

Let's first get started with a review of the Ivy 5 model.

EXPLORING A SIMPLE EQUAL-WEIGHT FIVE ASSET CLASS MODEL

The Ivy 5 concept is premised on simplifying the asset-allocation problem, which, as a general principle, is backed by empirical evidence. For example, Victor Demiguel and his colleagues have explored many sophisticated methodologies to optimize asset allocation.[1] They have solutions that can possibly beat an equal-weight allocation, but these alternative solutions add a high degree of complexity. We've discussed the empirical rational for following a simple asset allocation model in Chapter 6. An equal-weight portfolio—also promoted by DeMiguel et al.—is what we recommend.

A few quotes attributed to Albert Einstein sum up the key lessons learned from piles of disinterested research compiled on the subject of asset allocation.

1. Keep it as simple as possible, but not simpler.
2. If you can't explain it simply, you don't understand it well enough.

The Ivy 5 portfolio includes five asset classes, each given an equal-weight allocation of 20 percent, as shown in Figure 9.1:

- SP500 = S&P 500 Total Return Index (US stocks)
- EAFE = MSCI EAFE Total Return Index (international stocks)
- REIT = FTSE NAREIT All Equity REITS Total Return Index (real estate)
- GSCI = GSCI Index (commodities)
- LTR = Merrill Lynch 7–10 year Government Bond Index (bonds)

At a high level, one can think of the Ivy 5 portfolio as 40 percent equity, 40 percent real assets, and 20 percent fixed income portfolio. We consider it a goldilocks portfolio: Not too simple; not too complex; just right.

On the risk-management front, the Ivy 5 portfolio leverages a simple moving average rule. We explored this trading rule, as well as time series momentum (TMOM), in Chapter 7. The simple moving average trading rule can be used across asset classes. Figure 9.2 is a diagram of how the Ivy 5 with a moving average rule might look in practice.

The Ivy 5 Concept				
Domestic Equity	International Equity	Real Estate	Commodities	Fixed Income
20%	20%	20%	20%	20%

FIGURE 9.1 Allocation under the Ivy 5 Concept

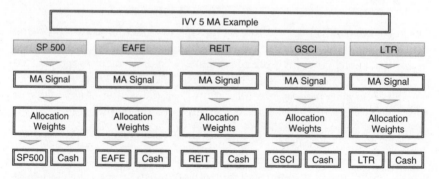

FIGURE 9.2 Ivy 5 with a Moving Average Rule

Ivy 5 with Moving Average Historical Performance

Our historical simulated time period is from January 1, 1976, to December 31, 2014, which is the longest period over which we can get data on the Ivy 5 asset classes. Results are gross of management fee and transaction costs. These are simulated performance results and do not reflect the returns an investor would actually achieve. All returns are total returns and include the reinvestment of distributions (e.g., dividends). Data are from Bloomberg and publicly available sources. Portfolios are annually rebalanced and the moving average rule is applied on a monthly basis. If an asset class is above its 12-month moving average at the end of the month, we maintain the position; otherwise, we sell the asset class and buy Treasury bills.

The following five asset classes are used in the backtest (referred to as the Ivy 5; see Table 9.1):

- SP500 = SP500 Total Return Index
- EAFE = MSCI EAFE Total Return Index
- REIT = FTSE NAREIT All Equity REITS Total Return Index
- GSCI = GSCI Index
- LTR = Merrill Lynch 7–10 year Government Bond Index[2]

Benchmark Summary Statistics Ten-year Treasury bonds (LTR) and US stocks (as represented by the S&P 500 Total Return Index) have performed well over the past 35 years. It is not surprising that market participants are so enamored with the 60/40 portfolio (60 percent US stocks or S&P 500, and 40 percent US bonds or LTR).

TABLE 9.1 Benchmark Summary Statistics

	SP500	EAFE	REIT	GSCI	LTR
CAGR	11.74%	9.57%	14.02%	5.50%	8.56%
Standard Deviation	15.01%	17.04%	17.02%	19.15%	8.36%
Downside Deviation (MAR = 5%)	11.01%	12.09%	14.48%	13.53%	5.21%
Sharpe Ratio	0.50	0.34	0.58	0.12	0.45
Sortino Ratio (MAR = 5%)	0.66	0.47	0.67	0.16	0.69
Worst Drawdown	−50.21%	−56.68%	−68.30%	−69.39%	−20.97%
Worst Month Return	−21.58%	−20.18%	−31.67%	−28.20%	−8.41%
Best Month Return	13.52%	15.58%	31.02%	22.94%	15.23%
Profitable Months	62.61%	59.83%	63.68%	56.62%	64.10%

Strategy Summary Statistics   In Table 9.2 we depict the simple Ivy 5 portfolio, the Ivy 5 portfolio with a moving average rule applied, a 60/40 portfolio, and an S&P 500 portfolio.

- IVY5_MA: five assets, equal-weight, annually rebalance
- 60/40: 60% SP500; 40% LTR, annually rebalance

Some quick takeaways: A 60/40 portfolio performed well, and the Ivy 5 portfolio with a moving average rule is tough to beat.

Unfortunately, we can't buy Ivy 5 index returns—we can only backtest them. Investment vehicles cost money in the real world, so we need to choose wisely. To replicate the Ivy 5, we could do the following with iShares products, which happen to have an ETF for all of the Ivy 5 exposures:

- IVV (7bps): iShares Core S&P 500
- EFA (34bps): iShares MSCI EAFE Total Return Index
- IYR (46bps): iShares US Real Estate
- GSG (75bps): iShares S&P GSCI Commodity-Indexed Trust
- IEF (15bps): iShares 7–10 Year Treasury Bond

In our previous analysis, we looked at gross of fee performance, but we clearly can't invest in an index for free. Using iShares, the ETF fee costs are 35.4bps, on average, plus transaction costs and RIA fees.

All that said, one could certainly implement the Ivy 5 with moving average strategy with minimal brain damage. Yahoo Finance charting allows you to run a monthly 12-month moving average test for each asset class, and with a yearly rebalance across asset classes, you would be in DIY heaven.

But can we do better.

TABLE 9.2   Strategy Summary Statistics

	IVY5	IVY_MA	60/40	SP500
CAGR	10.92%	10.98%	10.91%	11.74%
Standard Deviation	10.04%	7.35%	10.03%	15.01%
Downside Deviation (MAR = 5%)	8.66%	5.84%	6.92%	11.01%
Sharpe Ratio	0.61	0.80	0.61	0.50
Sortino Ratio (MAR = 5%)	0.68	0.98	0.85	0.66
Worst Drawdown	−45.32%	−12.65%	−25.29%	−50.21%
Worst Month Return	−19.48%	−10.37%	−13.14%	−21.58%
Best Month Return	8.59%	7.37%	9.70%	13.52%
Profitable Months	68.80%	72.22%	65.60%	62.61%

At the outset we mentioned that the Ivy 5 allocation concept coupled with a moving average rule is a reasonable solution. However, we also mentioned that we can improve on this model by focusing on our portfolio mission, introducing security selection, and enhancing the risk-management system. We explore each of these issues as follows.

ENHANCING THE IVY 5 CONCEPT

Improving Security Selection and Risk-Management

We explored risk-management and security selection in Chapters 7 and 8, respectively. The evidence from Chapter 7 suggested that we consider a combination of simple moving averages and time-series momentum trading signals to help us avoid massive drawdowns. This blended concept we labeled as the ROBUST approach. In Chapter 8, the evidence suggested that introducing focused exposures to value and momentum can be beneficial to a portfolio, relative to market-cap-weighted passive indices. Logically, we should be able to integrate these findings into a coherent portfolio approach that can build on the Ivy 5 framework.

Of course, adding complexity to a simple model is hazardous to one's wealth, and we must tread carefully. We present three concepts that integrate our research findings into an asset allocation framework. We provide three options, because every investor is different. The first thing we asked in this chapter is, "What is your portfolio's mission?" and since this can be different for a 30-year-old compared to an 80-year-old, we present three options. They are meant to suffice for a wide swath of investors whose primary goal is to protect against inflation, preserve capital, and grow their real wealth.

But perhaps you are an investor with an extremely bearish view on bonds? Or perhaps you are extremely bullish on equities? Or maybe you think the value anomaly is a fraud? As an investor, who has earned his or her hard-earned wealth, you maintain the right to allocate as you see fit. Go for it. We merely present the three options as a reasonable solution to a complex problem (we allow the equity portion to be either 40%, 60%, or 80%):

We explain the process outlined in Figure 9.3:

Step 1 in the DIY process is to replace generic passive allocations to domestic and international equity with high-conviction tax-efficient value and momentum alternatives.

Step 2 in the process is to calculate moving average (MA) and time-series momentum (TMOM) risk-management calculations on each "line" of the system (e.g., REITs, Domestic Value, etc.). If both the TMOM

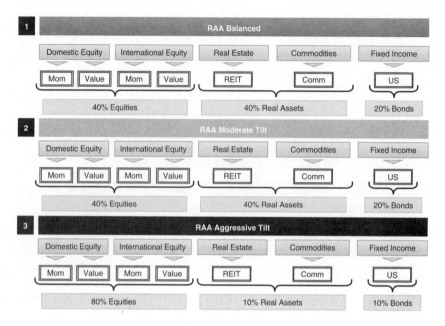

FIGURE 9.3   Three DIY Concepts

and MA rules say to be in an asset class, we are 100 percent long this asset. If both the TMOM and MA rules say to be out of an asset class, we move to Treasury Bills for this asset class. If the rules say different things for an asset class (TMOM says to buy while MA says to sell, or vice versa), we are 50 percent long this asset, and 50 percent in Treasury Bills.

Step 3 in the process involves the implementation of tax-management techniques. One option is to embed the system in an exchange-traded fund (ETF), where tax liability can be minimized; alas, most DIY investors don't have the capability to launch an ETF. However, for the DIY investor, they can harvest short-term losers; tax-manage hedging events by shorting exposures that are highly correlated; and by annually rebalancing, such that one maximizes long-term capital gains and minimizes short-term capital gains. If an investor is running this system across qualified and nonqualified accounts, concentrate taxable dollars in tax-efficient equity exposures; concentrate nontaxable dollars in tax-inefficient fixed income and real asset exposures. For the analysis that follows, we conduct a annually rebalance. We do not tabulate annual results; however, we note that they are quantitatively similar.

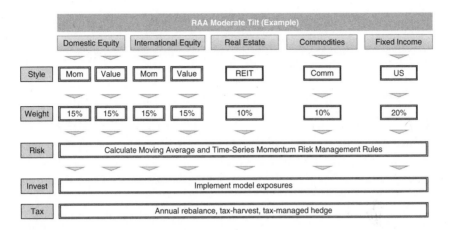

FIGURE 9.4 DIY Moderate Tilt (Example)

Figure 9.4 outlines how this process might look if we selected a "moderate" tilt strategy.

How Does the DIY Solution Perform?

Our simulated time period is from January 1, 1992, to December 31, 2014 (limited due to international data limitations).[3] Benchmark and strategy results are gross of management fee and transaction costs for illustrative purposes only. One would want to consider the effects of transaction costs and taxes when deploying this strategy in a real-world environment. All returns are total returns and include the reinvestment of distributions (e.g., dividends). Portfolios are annually rebalanced. MA and TMOM risk-management rules are applied on a monthly basis.

The following nine asset classes are used in the study that follows:

- SP500 = SP500 Total Return Index
- EAFE = MSCI EAFE Total Return Index
- REIT = FTSE NAREIT All Equity REITS Total Return Index
- GSCI = GSCI Index (commodities)
- LTR = Merrill Lynch 7–10 year Government Bond Index[4]
- Simple Value = Top decile of US firms sorted on EBIT/TEV as described in Chapter 8
- Simple MOM = Top decile of US firms sorted on past Momentum as described in Chapter 8

- Simple Int'l Value = Top decile of International firms sorted on EBIT/TEV as described in Chapter 8
- Simple Int'l MOM = Top decile of International firms sorted on past Momentum as described in Chapter 8

Benchmark Summary Statistics We first examine the performance of simple momentum and value portfolios relative to buy-and-hold market-cap weighted portfolios (the details on the construction of these portfolios are outlined in Chapter 8). The results in Table 9.3 show that domestic value and momentum clearly outperform the buy-and-hold index over the 1992 to 2014 time period (these strategies also outperform in prior periods). These summary statistics are presented gross of fees, and realized returns would definitely be lower for active strategies—especially momentum, which is rebalanced monthly. However, as noted in Table 9.3, the simple momentum and simple value strategies have earned returns that are 4 percent per year higher than the benchmark. As long as an investor can minimize transaction fees, asset management costs, and tax drag associated with these more active strategies, there is an opportunity to add value to a portfolio by a diligent DIY investor focused on the FACTS.

In Table 9.4 we conduct the same analysis outlined above, but for international stocks (again, details on the construction of these portfolios are outlined in Chapter 8). Once again, simple value and momentum strategies outperform the buy-and-hold index by a wide margin. As was the case previously, the trick for the DIY investor is in identifying ways to minimize transaction costs, management fees, and taxes in the quest to capture the spread between value and momentum and the general market. In practice, more advanced value and momentum screening methodologies can increase expected returns, but those methodologies are beyond the scope of this book.[9]

TABLE 9.3 Domestic Equity Summary Statistics (1/1992–12/2014)

	SP500	Simple Value	Simple MOM
CAGR	9.58%	15.59%	14.85%
Standard Deviation	14.38%	16.97%	26.95%
Downside Deviation (MAR = 5%)	10.92%	13.54%	18.27%
Sharpe Ratio	0.52	0.78	0.55
Sortino Ratio (MAR = 5%)	0.48	0.81	0.68
Worst Drawdown	−50.21%	−47.33%	−58.40%
Worst Month Return	−16.70%	−20.67%	−28.17%
Best Month Return	10.93%	13.77%	42.73%
Profitable Months	64.49%	65.22%	63.04%

TABLE 9.4 International Equity Summary Statistics (1/1992–12/2014)

	EAFE	Simple Int'l Value	Simple Int'l MOM
CAGR	5.39%	12.32%	10.92%
Standard Deviation	16.50%	17.12%	19.66%
Downside Deviation (MAR = 5%)	12.10%	12.91%	15.06%
Sharpe Ratio	0.24	0.61	0.49
Sortino Ratio (MAR = 5%)	0.14	0.63	0.49
Worst Drawdown	−56.68%	−55.71%	−55.26%
Worst Month Return	−20.18%	−23.05%	−20.67%
Best Month Return	12.80%	19.23%	16.33%
Profitable Months	58.70%	64.13%	62.32%

TABLE 9.5 Real Assets and Bonds Summary Statistics (1/1992–12/2014)

	REIT	GSCI	LTR
CAGR	11.61%	1.51%	7.16%
Standard Deviation	19.23%	20.96%	6.03%
Downside Deviation (MAR = 5%)	16.59%	15.06%	3.86%
Sharpe Ratio	0.53	0.05	0.73
Sortino Ratio (MAR = 5%)	0.48	-0.08	0.55
Worst Drawdown	−68.30%	−69.39%	−6.78%
Worst Month Return	−31.67%	−28.20%	−5.71%
Best Month Return	31.02%	19.67%	8.73%
Profitable Months	62.68%	55.43%	65.22%

Table 9.5 provides the summary statistics for the real asset categories—commercial real estate and commodities—and government bonds. Over the time period examined, bonds have been the best risk-adjusted performers, which is not surprising given the dramatic drop in interest rates over this period. One could argue that lower interest rates also supported a nice run in REITs over this time period. Commodities, proxied by GSCI, had the worst run over this time period. In practice, we would likely avoid a GSCI-based commodity exposure, which is suboptimal relative to commodity exposures that exploit commodity term-structure and momentum premiums. That said, for data availability purposes, the GSCI index serves as a reasonable proxy for commodity exposure.

Asset Allocation Summary Statistics (without Risk Management) Before exploring the DIY concept with risk-management, we first examine the performance of our asset allocation model infused with security selection benefits (as discussed in Chapter 8). We generate results for the three permutations of the asset allocation solution presented in Figure 9.3 (Balanced, Moderate, and Aggressive). In the analysis the follows, the definitions for each strategy are outlined as follows:

- DIY_BAL = 40% Equity (10% US Value, 10% US Momentum, 10% international Value, 10% international Momentum); 40% Real (20% commodities, 20% real estate); 20% Bonds.
- DIY_MOD = 60% Equity (15% US Value, 15% US momentum, 15% international Value, 15% international Momentum); 20% Real (10% commodities, 10% real estate); 20% Bonds.
- DIY_AGG = 80% Equity (20% US Value, 20% US momentum, 20% international Value, 20% international Momentum); 10% Real (5% commodities, 5% real estate); 10% Bonds.
- IVY5 = 40% Equity (20% S&P 500, 20% EAFE); 40% Real (20% commodities, 20% real estate); 20% Bonds.
- 60/40 = 60% Equity (S&P 500); 40% Bonds.

Table 9.6 summarizes the performance statistics for the three versions of the asset allocation system, the Ivy 5, and the buy and hold 60/40 portfolio. Results are shown gross of any transaction or management fees and include the reinvestment of dividends. None of the strategies deploy a risk-management overlay and all the strategies are annually rebalanced to their target weights.

TABLE 9.6 Strategy Summary Statistics (1/1992–12/2014)

	DIY_BAL	DIY_MOD	DIY_AGG	IVY5	60/40
CAGR	10.92%	12.25%	13.38%	8.23%	9.23%
Standard Deviation	11.53%	12.17%	14.47%	10.48%	8.47%
Downside Deviation (MAR = 5%)	10.20%	10.06%	11.53%	9.42%	6.09%
Sharpe Ratio	0.72	0.79	0.76	0.55	0.77
Sortino Ratio (MAR = 5%)	0.60	0.73	0.75	0.37	0.69
Worst Drawdown	−45.85%	−42.68%	−47.16%	−45.32%	−25.29%
Worst Month Return	−20.43%	−18.37%	−19.69%	−19.48%	−9.50%
Best Month Return	8.33%	8.70%	10.70%	8.59%	7.12%
Profitable Months	67.39%	67.03%	66.67%	66.30%	67.03%

The three asset-allocation models we propose all outperform that Ivy 5 portfolio on a risk-adjusted basis (e.g., as measured by Sharpe and Sortino ratios). This outperformance is driven by the benefits of security selection associated with exploiting the value and momentum effects. On a capital preservation basis, as measured by worst drawdown, the 60/40 portfolio performs the best. This drawdown protection is driven by the 40 percent exposure to long bonds, during a period in which the long bond had exceptional performance and drawdown characteristics. We also conducted an "apples to apples" comparison (results not tabulated) where we set the bond exposure to 40 percent on the DIY and Ivy 5 models. DIY outperforms the 60/40 portfolio on both a risk-adjusted basis and on a capital preservation basis, accentuating the benefit of adding security selection to an asset allocation model.

DIY Strategy Summary Statistics: Adding Risk Management Here we examine the performance of our do-it-yourself (DIY) model infused with security selection benefits (Chapter 8) and a more robust risk management platform that exploits both simple moving averages and time-series momentum (referred to as ROBUST in Chapter 7). We generate results for the three permutations of the DIY solution presented in Figure 9.3. In the analysis that follows, the definitions for each strategy are outlined:

- DIY_BAL_RM = 40% Equity (10% US Value, 10% US Momentum, 10% international Value, 10% international Momentum); 40% Real (20% commodities, 20% real estate); 20% Bonds. Risk-managed with ROBUST.
- DIY_MOD_RM = 60% Equity (15% US Value, 15% US momentum, 15% international Value, 15% international Momentum); 20% Real (10% commodities, 10% real estate); 20% Bonds. Risk-managed with ROBUST.
- DIY_AGG_RM = 80% Equity (20% US Value, 20% US momentum, 20% international Value, 20% international Momentum); 10% Real (5% commodities, 5% real estate); 10% Bonds. Risk-managed with ROBUST.
- IVY5_MA = 40% Equity (20% S&P 500, 20% EAFE); 40% Real (20% commodities, 20% real estate); 20% Bonds. Risk-Managed with a Moving Average rule.
- 60/40 = 60% Equity (S&P 500); 40% Bonds.

Table 9.7 summarizes the performance statistics for the three versions of the DIY system, the Ivy 5 with moving average system, and the buy-and-hold 60/40 portfolio. We assume that if we move into cash, we receive the risk-free rate of return (90-day T-bills). Results are shown gross

TABLE 9.7 Strategy Summary Statistics (1/1992–12/2014)

	DIY BAL_RM	DIY MOD_RM	DIY AGG_RM	IVY5 MA	60/40
CAGR	11.09%	12.02%	13.10%	9.29%	9.23%
Standard Deviation	7.87%	8.86%	10.84%	6.68%	8.47%
Downside Deviation (MAR = 5%)	5.77%	6.44%	8.04%	4.92%	6.09%
Sharpe Ratio	1.03	1.02	0.94	0.96	0.77
Sortino Ratio (MAR = 5%)	1.02	1.06	0.99	0.84	0.69
Worst Drawdown	−13.93%	−13.81%	−16.39%	−12.65%	−25.29%
Worst Month Return	−7.96%	−9.89%	−13.35%	−7.08%	−9.50%
Best Month Return	6.63%	8.53%	10.57%	5.48%	7.12%
Profitable Months	71.01%	69.93%	69.20%	69.93%	67.03%

of any transaction or management fees and include the reinvestment of dividends. All the strategies are annually rebalanced to their target weights and risk-management rules are applied on a monthly basis.

On a risk-adjusted basis, the three DIY strategies are roughly equivalent. They each generate a Sharpe ratio around one and a Sortino ratio comfortably above one. The metrics for the DIY systems are all favorable relative to the Ivy 5 and the 60/40 systems. A quick look at the worst drawdown statistic suggests that all of the strategies are favorable to a buy-and-hold strategy fully invested in equity: diversification clearly matters. We also notice that the trend following overlays on both the Ivy 5 (MA) system and the DIY system (MA and TMOM) dramatically reduce max drawdowns. This implies that trend-following rules, at least over this sample period, helped to blunt extreme loss scenarios.

Out-of-Sample Performance The evidence presented suggests that a DIY framework is more effective than either the Ivy 5 or 60/40 concept. However, the period we analyze—1992 to 2014—is short in nature. We want to be careful not to extrapolate the performance associated with DIY into the future. To contextualize the outperformance of DIY, we must ask two questions:

- What drove the DIY outperformance?
- Do we believe the drivers of outperformance will continue to be effective in the future?

DIY outperformance relative to the Ivy 5 concept was driven by a combination of security selection (value and momentum—shown in Table 9.6)

TABLE 9.8   Strategy Summary Statistics (1/1976–12/1991)

	DIY BAL_RM	DIY MOD_RM	DIY AGG_RM	IVY5 MA	60/40
CAGR	15.27%	15.58%	16.08%	13.46%	13.38%
Standard Deviation	8.25%	9.15%	10.65%	8.20%	11.91%
Downside Deviation (MAR = 5%)	7.83%	8.79%	9.91%	7.15%	7.90%
Sharpe Ratio	0.82	0.78	0.73	0.63	0.46
Sortino Ratio (MAR = 5%)	1.23	1.14	1.07	1.12	1.05
Worst Drawdown	−12.03%	−15.17%	−18.49%	−11.06%	−19.46%
Worst Month Return	−11.55%	−14.37%	−17.38%	−10.37%	−13.14%
Best Month Return	7.23%	8.97%	11.00%	7.37%	9.70%
Profitable Months	78.13%	78.13%	76.56%	75.52%	63.54%

and an enhanced risk management concept (adding TMOM alongside MA—shown in Table 9.7). We explored the robustness of our security selection enhancements and our risk-management system in Chapters 7 and Chapters 8. Both of these features performed admirably in periods prior to 1992. While one can never be certain, it seems reasonable to hypothesize that a DIY approach would have outperformed in an out-of-sample period prior to 1992. Unfortunately, we do not have the data on international value and momentum to confirm this hypothesis. However, we can conduct a quasi out-of-sample test from 1976 to 1991 by replacing the international value and momentum exposures with a generic passive index exposure (i.e., MSCI EAFE Total Return Index). We present our findings in Table 9.8. Similar to Table 9.7, we assume that if we move into cash, we receive the risk-free rate of return (90-day T-bills). Results are shown gross of any transaction or management fees and include the reinvestment of dividends.

The findings in Table 9.8 highlight the robustness of the modified DIY system. The DIY portfolios outperform the other alternatives out of sample. That said, all of these solutions are strong: The Ivy 5 and the 60/40 portfolio continue their strong performance with strong annual growth rates and risk-adjusted statistics.

FINISH STRONG: THE ULTIMATE DIY SOLUTION

Thus far, we've outlined a solid approach to managing a pool of capital. Our solution is highly sophisticated, but not overly complex. We've taken a baseline diversified portfolio construct (i.e., the Ivy 5), added some well-established security selection benefits (value and momentum), and applied some robust market-timing mechanisms to risk-manage the DIY portfolio. Aren't we finished? Yes and no. On one hand, any of the solutions already presented are reasonable approaches to managing a portfolio. This includes the simple 60/40 portfolio, the slightly more complex Ivy 5 portfolio, and the sophisticated, yet simple, DIY solution just presented. But we can make our DIY solution even better.

So far we have not applied simple, evidence-based active techniques to three asset classes: bonds, real estate (REITs), and commodities. For our bond exposure, we use the US 10-year Treasury index. This is one exposure where getting "cutesy" can get you in trouble. While there are certainly some sophisticated bond strategies that can increase returns, we are going to keep this exposure simple. Good, old-fashioned US Treasury bonds—or whatever asset one believes to be the global flight-to-quality asset—serve as a unique insurance-like asset for a portfolio. We consider the US Treasury bond to be "insurance-like" based on evidence, not conjecture. Consider the results in Table 9.9, which show the top 20 drawdowns of the S&P 500 from January 1, 1927, until December 31, 2014. We map the performance of the 10-year Treasury index (LTR) over the same period as the S&P 500

TABLE 9.9 Strategy Summary Statistics (1/1927–12/2014)

Rank	Date Start	Date End	S&P 500	LTR
1	8/30/1929	5/31/1932	−84.59%	13.55%
2	10/31/2007	2/28/2009	−50.21%	20.55%
3	8/31/2000	9/30/2002	−44.41%	33.46%
4	12/31/1972	9/30/1974	−42.73%	−6.05%
5	8/31/1987	11/30/1987	−29.58%	2.55%
6	11/30/1968	6/30/1970	−29.23%	−8.02%
7	12/31/1961	6/30/1962	−22.33%	3.97%
8	5/31/1946	11/30/1946	−22.17%	−0.71%
9	11/30/1980	7/31/1982	−16.53%	17.87%
10	1/31/1966	9/30/1966	−15.79%	−0.18%
11	6/30/1998	8/31/1998	−15.18%	3.70%
12	7/31/1957	12/31/1957	−15.13%	8.86%
13	5/31/1990	10/31/1990	−14.82%	3.59%
14	12/31/1976	2/28/1978	−14.46%	−1.45%
15	7/31/1956	2/28/1957	−9.90%	−0.65%
16	2/29/1980	3/31/1980	−9.75%	−3.15%
17	8/31/1978	10/31/1978	−9.43%	−3.04%
18	12/31/1952	8/31/1953	−9.01%	−1.66%
19	12/31/1959	4/30/1960	−8.42%	4.29%
20	8/31/1986	9/30/1986	−8.32%	−2.07%

drawdown. In addition to providing a real return, plus an expected inflation return, the US Treasury bond serves as a quasi-insurance policy: When stock markets blow up, US long bonds do well, on average. We know of no other asset class, besides managed futures strategies—which are expensive, complex, and beyond the capability of a DIY investor—that provide this type of performance during market-wide meltdowns. The US Treasury bond may be a tough sell during low nominal interest environments, but the proof is in the pudding: When the world turns upside down, investors come clamoring for safety. We recommend the DIY investor keep this exposure simple and to the point.

As highlighted above, when it comes to our bond exposure, "If it ain't broke, don't fix it." This sort of logic doesn't apply to real estate exposures. A large body of research suggests that there are systematic ways to improve on passive real estate investment exposures. For example, in a 2009 paper in the *Financial Analysts Journal* written by Derwall et al.,[10] they find that "REITs exhibit a strong and prevalent momentum effect that is not captured by conventional factor models." To verify this claim, we examine all REITs from the CRSP database with share code = 18 (REITs) as well as those listed on McKay Price's website, a professor who manually finds REIT matches in the CRSP and Compustat database to expand the universe.[11] We only examine REITs above the NYSE 40th percentile for market capitalization to avoid smaller REITs, which may skew results. Finally, we show results to an equal-weighted monthly-rebalanced portfolio of the top one-third of all REITs ranked on their past momentum over the past 12 months (ignoring last month's return).

We can also improve on a generic commodity exposure like GSCI, the Goldman Sachs Commodity Index. For example, research published in the *Journal of Finance* in 2014 by Szymanowska et al.[12] and research published in the *Journal of Banking & Finance* in 2010 by Fuertes et al.[13] find that commodity returns can be improved by sorting futures based on the term structure of the futures curve and the relative momentum of futures. To verify these results, we analyze a commodity strategy that sorts 22 commodity contracts each month on both backwardation and momentum. We then average these ranks, and go long the nine contracts with the highest average ranks.

We present our enhanced REIT and commodity strategies in Table 9.10. The results cover January 1, 1992, until December 31, 2014, due to limitations on our ability to get reliable commodity futures data and a large enough REIT sample to make the analysis worthwhile (we require a minimum portfolio size of 10). We highlight the legend below:

- REIT = FTSE NAREIT All Equity REITS Total Return Index
- REIT MOM = REIT Momentum strategy outlined above (from January 1, 1992, to December 31, 1994, we use the FTSE NAREIT Index).

TABLE 9.10 Strategy Summary Statistics (1/1992–12/2014)

	REIT	REIT MOM	GSCI	Alpha Commodities
CAGR	11.61%	14.22%	1.51%	13.61%
Standard Deviation	19.23%	17.90%	20.96%	15.06%
Downside Deviation (MAR = 5%)	16.59%	14.65%	15.06%	11.32%
Sharpe Ratio	0.53	0.69	0.05	0.75
Sortino Ratio (MAR = 5%)	0.48	0.68	−0.08	0.79
Worst Drawdown	−68.30%	−57.20%	−69.39%	−45.59%
Worst Month Return	−31.67%	−25.55%	−28.20%	−24.28%
Best Month Return	31.02%	18.12%	19.67%	14.90%
Profitable Months	62.68%	64.13%	55.43%	62.32%

- GSCI = GSCI Index (Passive Commodities)
- Alpha Commodities: Long the top nine commodity futures with the highest average ranking on backwardation and momentum.

As shown in Table 9.10, adding momentum to REITs adds nontrivial value to a portfolio. The REIT Momentum portfolio outperforms the passive REIT index on all measures. Also shown in Table 9.10, sorting commodity futures on backwardation and momentum greatly improves the performance of a commodity exposure relative to a passive commodity index such as GSCI.

So you might be wondering: What happens if we add improved REIT and commodity strategies to a DIY portfolio? We're about to find out. Here are the four strategies we tested from January 1, 1992, until December 31, 2014:

- Ultimate DIY = 60% Equity (15% US Value, 15% US Momentum, 15% international Value, 15% international Momentum); 20% Real (10% alpha commodities, 10% enhanced real estate); 20% Bonds. Risk-managed with ROBUST.
- DIY_MOD_RM = 60% Equity (15% US Value, 15% US Momentum, 15% international Value, 15% international Momentum); 20% Real (10% commodities, 10% real estate); 20% Bonds. Risk-managed with ROBUST.
- 60/40 = 60% Equity (S&P 500); 40% Bonds.
- SP500 = SP500 Total Return Index

The Ultimate DIY portfolio (shown in Table 9.11) wins on almost every metric: returns, risk, drawdowns, and so forth. Clearly, the Ultimate DIY

TABLE 9.11 Strategy Summary Statistics (1/1992–12/2014)

	Ultimate DIY	DIY MOD_RM	60/40	SP500
CAGR	13.08%	12.02%	9.23%	9.58%
Standard Deviation	8.80%	8.86%	8.47%	14.38%
Downside Deviation (MAR = 5%)	6.29%	6.44%	6.09%	10.92%
Sharpe Ratio	1.14	1.02	0.77	0.52
Sortino Ratio (MAR = 5%)	1.23	1.06	0.69	0.48
Worst Drawdown	−13.57%	−13.81%	−25.29%	−50.21%
Worst Month Return	−9.88%	−9.89%	−9.50%	−16.70%
Best Month Return	8.44%	8.53%	7.12%	10.93%
Profitable Months	69.93%	69.93%	67.03%	64.49%

portfolio is the best solution, historically. We've have to consider the costs of implementation, but the 4 percentage point spread in returns between the Ultimate DIY portfolio and a simple 60/40 portfolio gives a DIY investor a lot of wiggle room to add value. Of note, we find similar results hold for the other DIY portfolios (balanced and aggressive).

GET 'ER DONE

We recommend that DIY investors consider our DIY framework. We've presented some relatively simple models, which only require an investor to hold seven assets (all of which can be replicated via exchange-traded funds), and apply a simple risk-management overlay once a month! We even provide the weights for each asset class associated with the DIY solution on our website (AlphaArchitect.com) each month to help readers make this happen. The downside is that the DIY strategy presented is more complicated than a simple 60/40 allocation, but investors are leaving a lot on the table by being *too* simple. And if successful, DIY investors will be paying themselves the 1 percent a year (or more) they would have had to pay a financial advisor to advise them on their asset allocation. The only costs will be the fees associated with the underlying ETFs utilized and/or commissions paid on individual securities purchased.

Now, before you get too excited, as we move from theory to practice, we need to consider the FACTS when selecting exposures that will help us implement the DIY strategy. Understand the fees, the liquidity, the complexity, the taxes, and the due-diligence costs associated with each exposure. Table 9.12

TABLE 9.12 Suggested Vehicles to Deploy DIY

	Vehicle Recommended
Active Domestic Value	Active ETF, Less than 50 stocks, at least annually rebalanced
Active Domestic Momentum	Active ETF, Less than 50 stocks, at least quarterly rebalanced
Active International Value	Active ETF, Less than 50 stocks, at least annually rebalanced
Active International Momentum	Active ETF, Less than 50 stocks, at least quarterly rebalanced
REIT	Active ETF, Less than 50 REITs, at least quarterly rebalanced, momentum-focus
Commodities	ETF, ETN, term-structure and momentum focus
Bonds	ETF, ETN, low-cost passive focus

highlights the assets one might consider when implementing the DIY process. ETFs are preferred to mutual funds due to their tax efficiency, which is of utmost importance for taxable investors actively traded strategies. ETFs also have an edge over individual stock purchases because of the tax-efficiency. The benefit of individual stock purchase is the investor can avoid the fees attached to an ETF. ETNs are an interesting vehicle for commodities and bonds because of their enhanced tax-efficiency relative to ETFs. The downside of ETNs is they have potential counterparty risk issues. To keep things simple, we recommend finding ETF vehicles that give you exposure to passive Treasury bonds and exposures to commodity strategies that exploit term structure and momentum. The danger is that investors pay too much for active exposures, and/or buy closet-index exposures that don't actually give them the active exposure desired. However, as long as DIY investors consider the FACTS when determining their investments, and do their homework on the underlying vehicles they invest in, they can't go too wrong.

NOTES

1. See Victor DeMiguel, Raman Uppal, Yuliya Plyakha, and Grigory Vilkov, "Improving Portfolio Selection Using Option-Implied Volatility and Skewness," *Journal of Financial and Quantitative Analysis* 48, no. 6 (2013) and Victor DeMiguel, Lorenzo Garlappi, Francisco J. Nogales, and Raman Uppal, "A Generalized Approach to Portfolio Optimization: Improving Performance by Constraining Portfolio Norms," *Management Science* (March 6, 2009).

2. Prior to June 1982, we use data from Amit Goyal's website: http://www.hec.unil.ch/agoyal/docs/PredictorData2013.xlsx.

3. This is a short time period, and the results must be taken with a grain of salt, but this is the best we can achieve given data limitations.

4. Prior to June 1982, we use data from Amit Goyal's website: http://www.hec.unil.ch/agoyal/docs/PredictorData2013.xlsx.

5. Data are from Ken French's website, accessed December 31, 2014, http://mba.tuck.dartmouth.edu/pages/faculty/ken.french/data_library.html.

6. Ibid.

7. Ibid.

8. Ibid.

9. See Wesley R. Gray and Tobias E. Carlisle, Quantitative Value: A Practitioner's Guide to Automating Intelligent Investment and Eliminating Behavioral Errors (Hoboken, NJ: John Wiley & Sons, 2012) as an example.

10. Jeroen Derwall, Joop Huij, Dirk Brounen, and Wessel Marquering, "REIT Momentum and the Performance of Real Estate Mutual Funds," *Financial Analysts Journal* 65 (2009): 1–11.

11. http://www.mckayprice.com/research.html.

12. Marta Szymanowska, Frans de Roon, Theo Nijman, and Rob van den Goorbergh, "An Anatomy of Commodity Futures Risk Premia," *Journal of Finance* 69 (2014): 453–482.

13. Ana-Maria Fuertes, Joelle Miffre, and Georgios Rallis, "Tactical Allocation in Commodity Futures Markets: Combining Momentum and Term Structure Signals," *Journal of Banking and Finance* 34 (2010): 2530–2548.

CHAPTER 10

Some Practical Advice

"The greatest obstacle to being heroic is the doubt whether one may not be going to prove one's self a fool; the truest heroism is to resist the doubt; and the profoundest wisdom, to know when it ought to be resisted, and when it be obeyed."

—Nathaniel Hawthorne

Nathaniel Hawthorne's lesson is clear: Know when we can—and when we cannot—trust ourselves. Our book's central lesson is that investors should explore a do-it-yourself (DIY) solution, or at least move in that direction. Are we, in fact, prepared to enter the world of DIY? Chapters 1 through 5 gave us the knowledge that "expert" opinion is suspect. These chapters also gave us the confidence that experts can be beat by disciplined investors adhering to a simple model. Chapters 6 through 8 described asset allocation, risk-management, and security selection. Finally, Chapter 9 integrates these lessons into a complete DIY solution that can beat the experts. We think we are ready—let's do it!

But wait.

While there are many reasons to pursue a DIY investment program, we have also learned that the biggest challenge to any successful investment program is controlling our emotions. As Munger taught us, it is always best to invert the question to broaden our understanding. Applying this principle, we should not be asking: "Should we be DIY investors?" The real question is: "Why won't we become DIY investors?"

So before we conclude, we want to outline three reasons you may not become your own advisor, and list three reasons you may fail to implement a DIY approach. Our intent is not to discourage you, but simply to warn you of some behavioral flaws that might inhibit you from taking action!

THREE REASONS WE WILL NOT BE A DIY INVESTOR

Fear of Failure

"And it never failed that during the dry years the people forgot about the rich years, and during the wet years they lost all memory of the dry years. It was always that way."

—John Steinbeck

We may avoid a DIY solution because if we do it ourselves and screw it up, well, then we're idiots and should have known better. As Steinbeck points out in the quote above, a dry year is a dry year, and that's all people remember. This kind of reaction happens all the time.

Consider the football coach whose team has moved down to the opponent's 1-yard line. It is now fourth down. Should the coach go for the touchdown or settle for the field goal? Statistically, football coaches have been shown to opt for a conservative kick far more often than they should.[3] Why?

One theory is that coaches are risk averse, and being stopped on fourth down, even if it is a better bet, is very painful (even hazardous to one's career). As Bill Cowher, former head coach of the Steelers put it, "... That one time it doesn't work could cost your team a football game, and that's the thing a head coach has to live with ..."[4] If the team goes for it, fails to score, and loses the game, the coach "made" the wrong decision.

Hindsight is, after all, 20/20. It's easy to anticipate the criticism: "Why didn't you take the bird in the hand? You should have kicked the field goal!" Coaches may anticipate the worst case and the criticism and just kick the field goal, even though this might be a suboptimal decision. They certainly don't want to explain themselves at the next cocktail party.

For our nest eggs, we want to avoid a similar fate. If your DIY effort has a down year, you don't want to explain to your spouse why you fired the expensive advisor! Your silly model got it wrong. An expert with the experience and knowledge to forecast the future would have been a better choice.

By contrast, if we hire an expert and have a bad outcome, then we aren't the coach who made the bad call. Marital bliss is preserved and a simple firing/hiring of a new coach is in order. In this scenario, we can still attend our cocktail party. "Yeah, we hired this Armani-clad expert to manage our portfolio. He charged outrageous fees and underperformed the index, so we fired him. You should see this new guy though! He is also an Armani-clad expert, but he has slicked-back hair! He charges outrageous fees, but he has deep experience and qualitative insights. His recommendations are complex and proprietary, so I am sure they will work ..." Emotionally, failure is scary. It's harder to pursue an option, albeit an empirically sound one, for the fear of bearing the blame when markets turn sour.

Inertia Is Difficult to Overcome

"To do nothing is within the power of all men."

—Samuel Johnson

The status quo is powerful and our ability to transition to a DIY solution may be impossible. As the old saying goes, "If it ain't broke, don't fix it." The effect of passivity is powerful, since a mistake due to an action committed is more psychologically painful than a mistake produced by a failure to act. When we depart from a default option of sticking with what we already have, we are setting ourselves up for regret.

When we make a change or take an action that results in a loss of utility, the pain of the loss is more significant than gains of a similar magnitude. And as we know from prospect theory, losses hurt more than gains. In financial terms, people appear to be more sensitive to losses than they are to gains, and tend to be "loss averse."

We see this bias reflected in the *disposition effect*, whereby investors are prone to hold losing stocks for too long, since realizing the loss would be psychologically painful. This effect also drives what we refer to as procrastination, whereby we postpone taking action, deferring our experience of pain.

Thaler and Sunstein, in their book *Nudge*, have referred to status-quo bias as the "yeah, whatever" heuristic.[7] By failing to explicitly choose to act, we implicitly choose inaction. A conversation between a DIY investor in a conversation with Mr. Status Quo might go as follows:

> **Us:** "But I could reduce the fees on my account!"
> **MR. Status Quo:** "Yeah, whatever."
>
> **Us:** "But I could reduce taxes and enhance long-run returns!"
> **Mr. Status Quo:** "Yeah, whatever."
>
> **Us:** "But I could finally understand my investment strategy!"
> **Mr. Status Quo:** "Yeah, whatever."

Since Mr. Status Quo is so easy to get along with, one can see how inertia could make for a very compelling strategy in many cases.

Relationships Matter

"Relationships take up energy; letting go of them, psychiatrists theorize, entails mental work."

—Meghan O'Rourke

We've had an advisor for a while—maybe a long while—5 years, 10 years, or perhaps 20+ years. At this point, our advisor is a friend, and breaking up with friends is hard to do. But we must ask ourselves the following question: "How much is this friendship worth?" If an advisor is charging a 1 percent fee for the rest of our life, that is arguably equivalent to giving our advisor "friend" 10 percent of our current net worth on an annuitized basis. Is the friendship worth 10 percent of our current wealth? One would think not. And yet, firing an advisor is tough! Some people don't mind having "paid friends."

We also tend to trust our advisors like we trust our friends. And it is perhaps our oldest friends whom we trust the most. Similarly, it may be that the longer we have been working with our advisor, the more we trust him. Most investors consult with a financial advisor when making investment decisions. If someone has been doing something for a long time, then it stands to reason they must be good at it, or they wouldn't still be doing it.

Financial advisors are human. We prefer humans to machines. We can pick up the phone and speak with a human. We can speak to them about our emotions. We can talk to humans about our financial goals. We can talk to humans about our hopes and fears. We are biased to believe in and trust a human advisor relative to a mechanical advisor because humans are more like us. Is this preference justified? Let's examine it more closely.

When we make a decision, we consider not only how we think about it analytically but also how we feel about it, which can skew how we assess its risks. If we have positive or favorable feelings about an activity, we tend to magnify its benefits in our minds and reduce its perceived riskiness. Conversely, if we have negative or unfavorable feelings, we tend to ascribe higher risks to it and lower benefits. This is known as the *affect heuristic,* since our "affect," or the emotion we are feeling at the time, can influence our judgments. Although we often feel we are being rational in making our judgments, the affect heuristic influences us in profound ways that are directly related to our feelings, and not our rationality. This is not a good thing when it comes to making investment decisions.

But You Can Become a DIY Investor!

We have faith you can become a DIY investor. We simply want to point out some reasons, which lead to the status quo of outsourcing your investments – Fear of failure, Inertia, and Relationships.

Next we turn our attention to three mistakes that investors may make when they decide to go down the DIY route.

THREE REASONS YOU MIGHT FAIL

Omitted Facts and Figures Mislead

"There are as many opinions as there are experts."
—Franklin D. Roosevelt

Another reason we could fail to follow a DIY approach is that we have specific objections to some of the conclusions in this book. The allocations discussed could be insufficient, as these are not enough asset classes to provide appropriate diversification. Maybe we need 12, or 40, or 400. Or perhaps we believe that the road to wealth is to take a highly concentrated position in a few stocks, and just be sure that these stocks are bought with an adequate margin of safety. Maybe we should just hold dividend stocks, or stocks we "know" are high quality (Coca-Cola) or have huge growth potential (Tesla, anyone?). Additionally, some could think of find simple technical rules, and their use in preventing extreme drawdowns, as heresy. If moving average rules have not worked recently, they probably never work, right?

And why not hedge funds? Many believe there are good reasons to invest in hedge fund products. They provide a source of uncorrelated returns, and thus, diversification from the volatile markets we live with. It's also possible to identify the best managers as long as you are willing to incur the blood, sweat, and tears to research every single one. For some, the tax consequences, lock-up of capital, and fees of hedge funds can be managed. As for us, we don't like paying taxes, we like having access to our hard-earned wealth, and interviewing hedge fund managers all day isn't necessarily our favorite thing to do.

Our book also ignores the newest "innovations" on Wall Street that claim to exploit various advancements in portfolio management. There may be some merit lurking in these frontiers of finance; however, we simpletons like exactly that: keeping it simple. This book scratches the surface on these opportunities, but does not explore them in detail. For those with the resources and time to explore these opportunities, they may be viable.

Most importantly, let us not forget the qualitative aspects of investment and the value that some place in experience when it comes to finance. No matter what data we may find, or empirical evidence we can produce, some humans will always revert toward an "expert" opinion. A study of 250 seasoned investors determined that approximately two-thirds agreed with this statement: "As a forecasting task becomes more complex and difficult, I tend to rely more on judgment and less on formal, quantitative analysis."[2] If the experts leverage judgment and experience, shouldn't we do the same? Many continue to believe that experts beat simple models. The data certainly don't support this hypothesis, but as Wes's father used to say on their cattle ranch: "You can lead a horse to water, but you can't make him drink."

We want to warn potential DIY investors that the fully integrated investment approach we present in Chapter 9 is not perfect, but it is robust, and we believe the model works for a large group of investors seeking to preserve their capital and capture some upside. We've purposely left out many tests and results in this book, since including them would have made it unnecessarily long.

Overconfidence

> "Well, I think we tried very hard not to be overconfident, because when you get overconfident, that's when something snaps up and bites you."
>
> —Neil Armstrong

DIY is great for some people, but we aren't the average person. We're exceptional and have the confidence in our own ability to beat a model. Sure, the model can add value, but the model merely serves as a guideline and serves as a floor on our ability. However, with some extra effort, and of course skill, we can leverage the model and combine it with our ability to attain remarkable performance. The logic is as follows: Models have been shown to outperform humans, but if we were to use the model selectively, we could surely add value.

Let's take an example from value investing. As we demonstrated in Chapter 8, this has been a decent strategy. So let's say we run the model and come up with 50 stocks, which are classified as cheap or value stocks. We recommend equal-weighting these 50 stocks to get a diversified portfolio. However, we decide to read the annual financials from each company (10-Ks) and really think company X is the best buy. As opposed to following the model and putting 2 percent of our money into this company (equal-weight across 50 stocks), we decide that we are going to invest 100 percent in this one stock! After the stock has a 30 percent drawdown, we then add more money to this investment, as our overconfidence keeps growing! This is a dangerous game to play (and in general, a losing game, as all three of us can attest to). As this example illustrates, overconfidence in our own "edge" can be dangerous.

We want to warn potential DIY investors of becoming overconfident in one asset class and straying from the model. Even we have fallen into this trap in the past (before moving to a simple model)!

Everyone Wants to Be a Hero

"The toughest thing about success is that you've got to keep on being a success."

—Irving Berlin

We all want to be good investors. We want to show the world how talented we are. We want to demonstrate that we are not just better than average, but we are elite. We would like nothing better than to go on TV where people would ask our opinion about economics, investing, and the financial news of the day. We want our children to refer to us as being especially smart financially. Nothing would be better than if some day, far in the future, people would look back and say, "What a profoundly talented person he was." In short, everyone wants to be a hero. And why not? If we're a hero, we can feel good about ourselves.

Sadly, the truth hurts. And the truth is that not everyone can be a hero. This isn't little league baseball, and no, you don't get a trophy just for playing. In fact, very few can be heroes. Even worse, today's hero is often tomorrow's zero. Take a look at the big names in the hedge fund and mutual fund business. When it comes to making money by picking stocks, success is a fleeting phenomenon indeed. A few memorable "heroes" of stockpicking:

Bill Miller: Beat the S&P 500 for 15 years in a row, but got destroyed during the financial crisis, erasing essentially all of his outperformance over the prior 15-year period.

Julian Robertson: Possibly the best stock picker of all time, but was laid low by a poorly timed yen bet, another bad bet on US Air, and then the tech bubble; he liquidated his Tiger fund, which was down as much as 40 percent versus the S&P 500 in 1999.

John Paulson: Merger arbitrage specialist turned macro hedge fund manager. Spectacular gains betting on housing's collapse, followed by spectacular losses on gold and Europe.

We want to warn potential DIY investors to stop worrying about being a hero. Simply stick to the model, and let other people talk about their "heroic" individual stock picks. (These are probably the same people who *always* win money at the casinos!)

BUT DON'T LOSE HOPE!

Taking control of our portfolio sounds good on paper, but a DIY approach can be difficult. We must consider our process and understand reasons we may keep the status quo, and reasons we may fail. A simple model that keeps fees low, maintains liquidity, limits complexity, minimizes taxes, and avoids search costs can outperform the experts. Some of us may still prefer to work with an advisor, which makes sense if we know we do not have the mental discipline to adhere to the model. If we do decide to work with an advisor, stick to the FACTS, and remember that simple models can beat experts. Keep asking questions and make sure you understand each position in your portfolio.

However, we believe that many of us—from the middle-class to the mega-rich—can do it ourselves. Our financial health—and wealth—depend on it! We've outlined a DIY solution that can point us in the right direction. This concept is not the only DIY solution. There are many others. And we challenge everyone to develop their own concepts. In the end, as long as we are disciplined and committed to a thoughtful process that meets our goals, we will be successful as investors. Go forth and be one of the few, one of the proud, one of the DIY investors who took control of their hard-earned wealth. You won't regret the decision.

IS DIY THE ONLY SOLUTION?

We have tried to emphasize throughout this book that the FACTS matter. Armed with the FACTS framework, a DIY investor will naturally gravitate toward simple solutions that get the job done. As we saw throughout our analysis, a simple Ivy 5 or 60/40 solution can work well for the DIY investor. With our DIY solution, we've tried to add elements of asset allocation (simple is better), security selection (value and momentum seem to work), and an improved risk-management concept (trend-following and time-series rules) to create a portfolio "for all seasons." Perhaps the DIY solution might not be ideal for you. That's fine. But any portfolio management solution should be relatively simple, minimize complexity, and be robust across different market regimes. Simultaneous with these requirements, the solution must be affordable, liquid, simple, tax-efficient, and transparent—otherwise, many of the benefits of the solution will flow to advisors, asset managers, and Uncle Sam.

To help facilitate the DIY solution, our firm, Alpha Architect, has a set of free tools to facilitate much of the analysis conducted throughout this book. We encourage you to visit the site to learn more: AlphaArchitect.com. We provide this service because it is directly in line with our firm's mission: *To Empower Investors Through Education*. We will provide monthly signals for the risk-management rules to help investors stick to the model (simply go to our website each month)!

And while we have an inspirational mission and a strongly held belief that we can disrupt the financial services industry for the better, it is important to note that we are a for-profit enterprise and have vested interests. We want to be fully transparent on this point: While we encourage and facilitate DIY investors, our firm does implement the DIY approach for clients and we charge fees for these services.

More importantly, we sponsor active strategies that capture the value and momentum anomalies, and for executing these strategies we charge a fee. Our products are meant to provide the "plugs" for value and momentum exposures suggested in the DIY framework, or any framework that seeks to exploit value and momentum strategies. However, one can also implement these stock strategies via trading the individual stocks in their brokerage account, thus eliminating any management fees we might charge. We encourage DIY investors to take this approach if they want the challenge and are indifferent to taxes. For those less inclined to run an internal asset management firm, and for those with taxable assets, we believe our strategies are unique in that they are tax-efficient, affordable, and truly active (less than 50 stock portfolios).

We hope you enjoyed the book and explore our tools and our research. We welcome your feedback on how we can improve our tools and help empower investors through education.

NOTES

1. Jean-Louis Dessales, "Simplicity Theory" (September 9, 2014), http://www .simplicitytheory.org/.
2. Michael J. Mauboussin, *The Success Equation: Untangling Skill and Luck in Business, Sports, and Investing* (Boston: Harvard Business Review Press, 2012).
3. David Romer, *It's Fourth Down and What Does the Bellman Equation Say? A Dynamic-Programming Analysis of Football Strategy* (Berkley: University of California Press, 2003).
4. Greg Garber, "Fourth-Down Analysis Met with Skepticism," ESPN.com (October 31, 2014), http://static.espn.go.com/nfl/columns/garber_greg/1453717 .html.
5. Paul E. Meehl, *Clinical Versus Statistical Prediction: A Theoretical Analysis and a Review of the Evidence* (Brattleboro, VT: Echo Point Books & Media, 2013).
6. Jan Engelmann, C. Monica Capra, Charles Noussair, and Gregory S. Berns, "Expert Financial Advice Neurobiologically 'Offloads' Financial Decision-Making under Risk," *PLOS One* (March 24, 2009), http://www.plosone.org/article/ info:doi/10.1371/journal.pone.0004957.
7. Richard H. Thaler and Cass R. Sunstein, *Nudge: Improving Decisions About Health Wealth, and Happiness* (New York: Penguin Group, 2009).

Appendix: Analysis Legend

The following table provides a definition of the words and symbols we use in the book.

Word/Symbol	Description
DIY	Do-It-Yourself
ROBUST	50 percent TMOM; 50 percent MA
TMOM	Time series momentum
MA	Simple moving average
S&P 500	Standard & Poor's 500 Total Return Index, the free-float, market-capitalization-weighted index including the effects of dividend reinvestment
CAGR	Compound annual growth rate.
Standard Deviation	Sample standard deviation (annualized by square root of 12)
Downside Deviation	Sample standard deviation of all negative observations (annualized by square root of 12)
Sharpe Ratio	Monthly return minus risk-free rate divided by standard deviation (annualized by square root of 12)
Sortino Ratio (MAR=5%)	Monthly return minus minimum acceptable return (MAR/12) divided by downside deviation (annualized by square root of 12)
Worst Drawdown	Worst peak-to-trough performance
Worst Month Return	Worst monthly performance
Best Month Return	Best monthly performance
Profitable Months	Proportion of monthly performances that have a positive return

About the Companion Website

This book includes a companion website, which can be found at http://www.alphaarchitect.com. This website includes the following:

- A screening tool to find value and momentum stocks described in the book
- An asset-allocation backtesting tool
- A blog about recent developments in quantitative investing
- And much, much, more

About the Authors

Wesley R. Gray, PhD, has studied and been an active participant in financial markets throughout his career. After serving as a captain in the United States Marine Corps, Dr. Gray received a PhD, and was a finance professor at Drexel University. Dr. Gray's interest in entrepreneurship and behavioral finance led him to found Alpha Architect, LLC, an SEC-registered investment adviser, where he is the executive managing member. Dr. Gray has published two books: *EMBEDDED: A Marine Corps Adviser Inside the Iraqi Army* and *QUANTITATIVE VALUE: A Practitioner's Guide to Automating Intelligent Investment and Eliminating Behavioral Errors*. His work has been highlighted on CBNC, CNN, NPR, Motley Fool, WSJ Market Watch, CFA Institute, Institutional Investor, and CBS News. Dr. Gray earned an MBA and a PhD in finance from the University of Chicago and graduated magna cum laude with a BS from the Wharton School of the University of Pennsylvania.

John (Jack) R. Vogel, PhD, conducts research in empirical asset pricing and behavioral finance, and has collaborated with Dr. Gray on multiple projects. His dissertation investigates how behavioral biases affect the value anomaly. His academic experience involves being an instructor and research assistant at Drexel University in both the Finance and Mathematics department. Jack Vogel is currently a managing member of Alpha Architect, LLC, an SEC-registered investment adviser, where he heads the research department and serves as the chief financial officer. Jack has a PhD in finance and a MS in mathematics from Drexel University, and graduated summa cum laude with a BS in mathematics and education from the University of Scranton.

David P. Foulke is currently a managing member of Alpha Architect, where he assists in business development, firm operations, strategic initiatives, and developing papers on quantitative investing and behavioral finance topics. Prior to joining Alpha Architect, he was a senior vice president at Pardee Resources Company, a manager of natural resource assets, including investments in mineral rights, timber, and renewables. Prior to Pardee, he worked in investment banking and capital markets roles within the financial services industry, including at Houlihan Lokey, GE Capital, and Burnham Financial. He also founded two technology companies: E-lingo.com, an Internet-based provider of automated translation services, and Stonelocator .com, an online wholesaler of stone and tile. Mr. Foulke received an MBA from the Wharton School of the University of Pennsylvania, and an AB from Dartmouth College.

Index